EUROPEAN RECKONING

by E. Strauss

THE RULING SERVANTS*
COMMON SENSE ABOUT THE
COMMON MARKET*
IRISH NATIONALISM AND BRITISH DEMOCRACY*
SOVIET RUSSIA
SIR WILLIAM PETTY*
BERNARD SHAW: ART AND SOCIALISM

* *Also published in the United States of America*

EUROPEAN RECKONING

The Six
and
Britain's Future

E. STRAUSS

London
GEORGE ALLEN & UNWIN LTD
RUSKIN HOUSE MUSEUM STREET

Printed in Great Britain by
East Midland Printing Company Limited
Bury St. Edmunds, Kettering, Peterborough
and elsewhere in the UK

PREFACE

SINCE the publication of my book *Common Sense about the Common Market* at the beginning of 1958, the existence of the European Economic Community and the question of Britain's relationship with it has become the dominant issue of the day. The literature on the subject which, at least in the English-speaking world, was at that time barely a trickle, has become a flood; any new contribution should, therefore, indicate as clearly as possible which aspect of the problem it is dealing with, for it has become patently impossible to cover it as a whole in its bewildering complexity.

My earlier study was a political book on an economic subject. It was based on the conviction that the trend towards Western European concentration under Germany's economic leadership had led to a watershed in international relations, both economic and political, and that its true implications were woefully misunderstood by British official policy. I regarded the British counter-proposal for an industrial Free Trade Area as a gigantic irrelevance without a chance of success and proposed, as a practical alternative, the creation of a new preference area including all Commonwealth countries willing to merge their preferential arrangements with Britain in such a wider scheme.

Whether such a proposal would have fared any better than the policy pursued by the British Government, if it had been advocated at the time with the skill which the Six demonstrated in their own enterprise, cannot now be profitably discussed. The consolidation of the EEC, Britain's move into the blind-alley of the European Free Trade Association and the transformation of the American balance of payments position have clearly made it impossible of realization at present—and in the negotiations for Britain's entry into the EEC the existence of Commonwealth preference is proving a crucial factor in a very much less constructive way than I had in mind five years ago.

When the English and American editions of the book were exhausted, I decided, rather than bringing it up to date by more or less superficial references to the events of the recent past, to continue the analysis at the point at which it had been left off. Although both laborious and subject to all the handicaps inseparable from an attempt to analyse complex events while they are taking place, this seemed the only method likely to lead to a realistic assessment of the present situation; it also had the incidental advantage of testing the premises of the earlier work and the conclusions to which they had led.

The book now before the reader falls into two parts. The first two chapters are devoted to an attempt to recapitulate the history of the first four years of the European Economic Community which coincide with the first stage of the period of transition under the Treaty of Rome. This critical survey of the successes and failures of the Common Market, and the methods responsible for them, is bound to suffer from the limitations imposed on the outside observer without access to inside knowledge. In addition, it is no exaggeration to say that not even the full-time specialist could hope to read and digest in full the stream of facts and figures emanating from the various international bodies, and not least from the Six, without the backing of a well-equipped research organization. On the other hand, an independent assessment may derive some benefit from the absence of reticences and diplomatic embellishments inseparable from official and semi-official descriptions.

The first chapter shows the Six at work in building their European Community; in the second chapter a short analysis of the economic development of the member countries and their trading relations under the new regime has been undertaken. The literature on this subject, as distinct from the factual material, is as meagre as that on the institutions and achievements of the Community is abundant, although for an adequate understanding of the position it is of paramount importance.

The third chapter, which reviews the relations between the Community and its actual or potential associates, forms a natural link between the first part and the second part which is mainly devoted to the question of Britain's relationship to the Six.

In the opinion that, political considerations and American influence apart, official Britain is being propelled into this direction mainly by the economic difficulties of the country, I could not avoid a discussion of the root causes of Britain's economic *malaise*; however contentious, this diagnosis provides at least a coherent framework for putting and answering the question of the true relevance of Britain's projected membership of the EEC.

To deal with such a topical question between the hard covers of a book imposes certain limitations and presents compensating opportunities. At a time when every newspaper contains some item of new information of moves in and around Brussels, it would be idle to aim at keeping abreast of the fast-flowing stream of events. All that can be attempted is to provide a reasonably clear and consistent outline of the main course of development and of the decisive constellations of interests, which are inevitably blurred in day-by-day reporting, and to reformulate practical issues in the light of the long-term factors involved. The recent history of the Six, no less than the post-war dilemma of the British economy, thus prove directly relevant to the question of Britain's joining the Common Market—and both retain their significance irrespective of the final answer.

For reasons which will appear in the course of the argument, the study is virtually entirely concerned with economic problems, and its conclusions challenge directly what is widely regarded as the strongest part of the case in favour of British membership: the belief that the economic advantages of this step outweigh all other considerations. Although the matter is by no means exclusively economic in character—and in the course of the negotiations British entry into the EEC has emerged more and more as a primary aim of American diplomacy—the economic issue is crucial in the sense that for a country in Britain's position such a step would be clearly inadvisable, unless at least its economic effects are demonstrably favourable.

This approach differs admittedly from the attitude of many observers who regard the Common Market essentially as the creation of high-minded European Federalists which has, somewhat regrettably, become involved in such mundane matters as tariffs and trade. The most eminent exponent of this point of view is, perhaps, Lord Franks who explained to the shareholders of Lloyds Bank that 'no doubt there will be visits to the bargain basement during the negotiations and important matters will be discussed there—perhaps butter, or meat or wheat . . . but these issues are not in the end what the negotiations are about.' This olympian opinion of one of the most representative figures of post-war Britain—administrator, ambassador, bank chairman and university don—may well reflect in the most condensed form official Britain's lack of grasp of 'what the negotiations are about'; both in its appraisal of the real motive forces of the European Economic Community and in the truly political significance of the clash in basic trading patterns underlying differences on such everyday commodities as butter, meat or wheat.

The creation of the EEC may be regarded as the culmination and completion of the post-war era, the triumphant result of the economic reconstruction of Western Europe on traditional lines under American leadership and with American help, followed by a steadily more urgent Franco-German challenge to the American hegemony which had been accepted as a basic fact of modern life by official Britain. Nor should the possibility be entirely discounted that the great economic upsurge of 1959-62 was the end of a period of rapid expansion rather than a foretaste of even better things to come. Even the solemn commitment to rapid growth proclaimed on American initiative by the Organization for Economic Co-operation and Development (OECD) may be more characteristic of an era of incipient doubt than of effortless achievement. Although the official pronouncements of the EEC continue to express unshakable optimism, in the debates of the European Parliament the spectre of stagnation or recession is not so easily exorcised.

In the following discussion some use has been made of share indices as a reflection of complex social and economic processes. This was more a matter of necessity than of choice, for within the technical limits set to this study such indices, however crude, were the most suitable material available. However, there is no need to apologize too profusely for this procedure at a time when the movement of share prices has become one of the potentially most significant economic indicators.

June, 1962.   E. STRAUSS.

CONTENTS

PREFACE   *page*   7

I   THE SIX AT WORK
    1. Basic Conditions   13
    2. Trade and Finance   18
    3. Competition   30
    4. Establishment, Services and Transport   37
    5. Labour   41
    6. Agriculture   46

II THE COMMUNITY AND THE
    GREAT BOOM
    1. Output and Trade Patterns   57
    2. The Ill-Matched Partners   64
    3. The Economic Effects of Integration   83

III THE FORCE OF GRAVITY
    1. The Overseas Associates   94
    2. 'Good Neighbour' and 'Big Stick'   99
    3. Britain *versus* the Six   105

IV BRITAIN ON THE BRINK
    1. Hangover Policies   110
    2. Political Ends and Economic Means   125
    3. Economic Propaganda and Reality   130
    4. Basic Trade Patterns: Commonwealth
       and Agriculture   136
    5. The Real 'Entrance Fee'   146

V   REAL PROBLEMS AND SHAM
    SOLUTIONS
    1. The Issues for Britain   155
    2. Is there a Choice?   164
    3. The End of the Post-War Era   169

INDEX   174

I

THE SIX AT WORK

(1) BASIC CONDITIONS

THE strongly expansive and exhilarating force of prosperity during the past four or five years gave the co-operation of the Six the confident and optimistic outlook which is the result of success and one of its most effective guarantees. In this atmosphere the task of setting up the institutions of the Community and of making them work went on with speed and determination.

However, apart from the economic situation, a number of factors assisted the progress of the new venture. The most important amongst them were the community of the historical heritage of the Six, the similarity of the political balance and of the economic policy pursued by their governments and the experience of the European Coal and Steel Community (ECSC).

Although the immediate reaction to the collapse of Hitler's New Order in a welter of bloodshed and suffering was a wave of anti-German feeling of ferocious intensity, in the long run it was 'not just fortuitous' that 'the core of Europe' was formed by Germany, France, Italy and the Benelux countries. In the words of Professor Hallstein, the German President of the European Economic Commission, 'the area covered by the Communities is identical with the territory of those States which were brought to the edge of physical and political destruction by the wanton national-socialist adventure. This experiment has left in the hearts of these nations the fervent wish that such a thing shall never happen again'.[1] Despite its confident inaccuracy, this statement expresses an important fact. If it is arbitrary to exclude

[1] Dr Hallstein's speech in Aachen on May 11, 1961, on the occasion of receiving the Charlemagne prize. (*Bulletin of the EEC*, Brussels, May, 1961, p. 21.)

from the territory of Nazi occupation not only the even more savagely exploited and mutilated countries of Eastern and South Eastern Europe but also Austria, Denmark and Norway, it remains true that community of suffering under the Nazi heel was one of the forces moulding the new Western European grouping.

However, it is sufficient to mention the countries so arbitrarily forgotten in Dr Hallstein's peroration to appreciate the second factor, the similarity of political regime and economic policy pursued by the Six. For most of the post-war period, the ruling political party of the German Federal Republic, of the Fourth French Republic and of the Italian Republic were the Christian Democrats, closely allied with the Roman Catholic Church which was, perhaps, the strongest link between their sometimes rather discordant right and left wings. The political earthquake which destroyed the parliamentary regime in France and restored General de Gaulle to power introduced a new element into this natural *entente* without upsetting its underlying harmony—in the economic sphere it was, in fact, badly needed for its maintenance. In Belgium and the Netherlands broadly based 'great' coalitions including the local Labour party alternated with 'little' coalitions between the local equivalents of the Christian Democrats and the political representatives of certain sections of the business classes such as the Belgian Liberals.

The Labour and Socialist parties in the countries of the Six, whether in temporary office as in pre-Gaullist France or Benelux or in permanent opposition as in Dr Adenauer's Germany and (with the exception of a relatively small group) in Italy, at no time actively questioned the social and economic basis of post-war European society and were amongst the most ardent supporters of European integration in general and of the Common Market in particular. In practice they regarded the furtherance and protection of the special interests of the workers as their special task within the new institutions and loyally accepted the direction of the European Economic Community (EEC) by its dominant social forces. The latter had thus no need to waste a large part of their energies on internal struggles and could concentrate the better on the profitable business of making themselves at home within the wider framework of the Six and of finding empirical solutions to the inevitable conflicts of interests between their national constituents and their industrial components.

In this work they received considerable help from the accumulated experience of the ECSC which had, of course, served in many respects as a blueprint for the Rome Treaty and in others as a warning example. Despite its limited success, or rather its failure, as a method of genuine European integration, this organization provided through its five years of practical operation an invaluable proving ground for the techniques of a Six Nation Enterprise, including the creation of a joint assembly, civil service and legal system and the establishment of a body of procedural and judicial technique. The combined activities of the three European Communities—the EEC, the ECSC and Euratom—and the close co-operation between their separate organs provided excellent conditions for the full use of the lessons of the pilot scheme by its more ambitious and more significant successor.

Perhaps the most delicate task confronting an integrated multinational system is the allocation of offices amongst the nationals of its Member States. The easiest part of this problem is the fixing of national representations, although this can hardly be achieved without intricate bargaining. On the highest constitutional level this is contained in the Rome Treaty itself which regulates in detail the voting strength and procedure in the Council of Ministers, the Parliament (Assembly) and the Economic and Social Committee and, less directly, the national composition of the European Commission, while it intentionally refrains from prescribing national qualifications for the members of the Court of Justice. The necessity of ensuring a certain balance in other appointments, whether executive or consultative, is of course, all-pervading. This is by no means an obstacle to the creation of a genuine Community spirit but, on the contrary and only on the surface paradoxically, one of its essential conditions, for its success would be fatally prejudiced by the suspicion that one or the other of the Member States was usurping an unfair share of the available spoils of office.

The symmetry of interests in the operation of the system, though less obvious, is hardly less important than that of nationalities. In certain broad categories, national and economic factors are naturally combined; thus it is more than a coincidence that the President of the European Commission is a German, with a Frenchman—more acceptable to General de Gaulle than the previous holder of the office—in charge of Euratom which leaves the chairmanship of the Coal and Steel Community's High Authority rather incongruously in Italian hands. Within the European Commission it is again easy to see why a Dutchman is in charge of the Agricultural Department, an Italian of labour affairs and a Frenchman responsible for the Overseas Development Department. In the European Parliament, political affiliations on a six-country basis play a prominent part, while in the Economic and Social Committee the broad dividing line runs between employers, employees and 'others'.

Throughout the complex organization the proportional representation of different groups is carried out in a manner which ensures the factual predominance of the most powerful interests while guaranteeing to the junior partners their proper place and voice. This combination of hardheadedness and fairness is, of course, easier to achieve when things are going well than in times of crisis or depression and it is no patent recipe for the avoidance of serious clashes of interests, but it is all the same evidence of impressive political ability and has contributed not a little towards the successful launching of a difficult enterprise.

The Grand Design of the Rome Treaty

The building of the EEC involves two complementary operations: the removal of barriers and the forging of common economic and social policies.

To reduce or abolish obstacles to the free movement of manufactured goods, capital and labour is by no means a negative act, and the measures taken by the Six during the first stage of the transitional period in this field have much more than symbolic importance, because they have considerably increased the mobility of the two main factors of production as well as that of intra-Community trade. Apart from supplying a strong stimulus to economic activity, they have improved the institutional framework for the operations of modern business by widening its sphere of action and by spreading a psychological climate favourable to its progress.

This is, of course, entirely in line with the intentions of the creators of the Treaty and its basic purposes, but the Community would not have become a political reality, if its benefits had been reserved exclusively to the dominant business interests. The industrial interests of the Six, though in some respects natural allies, were in fact at no time a united phalanx, and in important details their aims were far from identical, partly due to differences in the economic development of the member countries and partly owing to the different balance of social and economic power in individual countries.

In order to safeguard the weaker partners, complex institutional and procedural arrangements would have been necessary in any case, for while important sections of the business community, particularly in Germany and Belgium, would have been satisfied with the sweeping away of the barriers inhibiting their expansion, the other powers could never have agreed to such a policy without substantial compensations. In addition, it would have been quite unacceptable to countries where other interests had a stronger say, chief amongst them the numerically most important sections of the population, the peasant-farmers and the industrial workers.

In the negotiations for the Treaty, these interests influenced the attitudes of different governments according to their relative strength. By and large, the German negotiating position was determined almost exclusively by the interests of finance and industry which also played the leading part in Belgium. France was preoccupied with safeguards for its large but relatively less highly developed industry, for the Welfare State of the fourth Republic, for its potentially enormously important agriculture and for its crumbling overseas empire. Italy, though strongly influenced by the pressure of its modern, if highly protected, industry in the North, tried to obtain the best possible terms for its agricultural export potential, its labour surplus and for its underdeveloped South, while in the Netherlands there was a superficially similar combination of industrial and agricultural interests on a much higher level of efficiency, though quantitatively on a smaller scale.

The Treaty of Rome was the resultant of these complex pressures of partly parallel but largely divergent interests. It represents a genuine compromise, even though its basic principles reflect the broad supremacy of the industrial business interests and, therefore, inevitably those of the strongest partner, the German Federal Republic. The way in which this balance of power is expressed in the Treaty is both curious and instructive: the agreements on the removal of obstacles to economic activities within the Community are as a rule detailed, specific and

B

subject to very definite time limits, while the qualifications safe-guarding other interests are embodied in broad programmes for the creation of a genuine economic union.

These qualifications include measures designed to keep the balance between the business classes of individual countries, such as the common external tariff (and a common commercial policy), the harmonization of economic and financial policy and the prevention of distortions in the flow of trade through the action of national governments; for the rest, the Community's positive policy is devoted to safeguards against the abuse of economic power by the dominant interests, to the promise of a joint transport policy and to the assurance of a new deal for labour and the rural population at home and of successful economic development for the overseas associates of the Six.

(2) TRADE AND FINANCE

The Common External Tariff

Art. 19 of the Treaty of Rome provides for a common customs tariff 'at the level of the arithmetical average of the duties applied in the four customs territories' (Benelux, France, Germany and Italy), generally with January 1, 1957, as the base, but subject to exceptions enumerated in seven separate lists attached to the Treaty itself.

At the time of its signature, agreement was still outstanding on a large number of sensitive commodities contained in List G to which some additions could still be made by each country. These rates were to be settled within two years or at least by the end of the first stage.

The Treaty also laid down the time table for the introduction of the common external tariff. The first step was to be taken after four years when the agreed rates would come into force for all items with a difference of 15% or less from the duties charged on January 1, 1957. Other rates would be adjusted by 30% of the difference (up or down), by a further 30% at the end of the second stage and the common tariff would completely enter into force at the latest by the end of the transitional period (art. 23). The most important escape clause allowed the grant of 'tariff quotas' free of duty or at reduced rates in cases where production in the Community was inadequate and a Member State depended traditionally on imports from abroad (art. 25).

The unexpectedly strong attacks on the EEC in GATT and the OEEC induced the Six to speed up agreement on the common tariff in order to present the outside world with a *fait accompli*, and the Commission pushed ahead vigorously with the technical preparations. The tariff positions where the rates were a simple average of existing duties were approved by the Council in February, 1960, and only a month later agreement was reached on the bulk of List G with the exception of seventy-two items 'representing less than 3% of tariff lines',[1] though a much higher share of the volume of trade, for they included such important commodities as petroleum products on which agreement is still outstanding. Most other matters except the duty on manufactured tobacco, which was not agreed until February, 1962, proved less stubborn: the problems of 'fiscal' customs duties, mixtures of specific and *ad valorem* rates and the tariff on newsprint were settled in 1960, and the 30% duty on unmanufactured tobacco in List F was supplemented by a levy which was further adjusted in July, 1961.

The common external tariff affects relations between the Member States as well as those between the Community and the outside world, and for this reason the first and rather halting step towards its introduction had to be taken a year earlier than anticipated as part of the so-called 'acceleration' programme. This step involved duty increases in Germany and Benelux which were followed by no fewer than 117 requests for tariff quotas by April, 1961; most of them came from the low-tariff group, but some quotas were also claimed and obtained by France and Italy.

The effect of these measures was a significant increase in the preferences granted to members of the Six at the expense of third countries, tempered by special temporary concessions to industries which would have suffered unduly from their introduction without delay. Whatever the precise balance of advantage at every single step, the hard bargaining at the beginning and the workmanlike solutions arrived at in almost all cases show the Community at its practical best—flexible in methods and reasonably fair to all the interests concerned which

[1] *EEC Third General Report on the activities of the Community* (1960), para. 35.

were, of course, mainly the business interests of the Six for whose benefit they were primarily designed.

Internal Duties and Quotas

The time table for the gradual removal of the barriers impeding the movement of goods between the Member States began earlier than that for the introduction of the common external tariff. An immense amount of thought and work had gone into the procedures for dealing with import duties and quantitative restrictions in the course of the transitional period of 12 (to 15) years divided into three stages. During the first 4(-6) years three duty reductions of 10 per cent each were to be made, the first 'across the board' affecting equally all rates in force on January 1, 1957, the others by rather more complex methods. The dates envisaged were the beginning of 1959, the middle of 1960 and the end of 1961.

For quotas, the Treaty provided that after one year all bilateral quotas should be made available to all member countries and increased by one fifth every year, subject to an initial minimum of three per cent 'of the national output' for all products subject to quantitative import restrictions; the minimum was to be increased to five per cent within two years, with further annual additions until the complete abolition of quota restrictions within the Community.

A complication was introduced into the arrangements by Western Germany, where the duties on most industrial products (except textiles and leather goods) had been reduced unilaterally by up to a quarter in the summer of 1957—before the Treaty came into operation but after the deadline for calculating duty levels. The declared purpose of this step had been a reduction in the mounting surplus of foreign exchange and the maintenance of stable prices; however, it was not only applied to imports from other Member States and may have owed something to Germany's desire to maintain its trade relations with third countries by reducing the amount of discrimination against their exports. In fact, the first two duty reductions under the Treaty of Rome established only insignificant preferences for the other Member States in the German market for industrial products.

In view of the sharp conflict between the Six and some other OEEC countries under British leadership at the time of the first reduction in duties in January, 1959, this was on certain conditions and in part extended to all member countries of GATT. (In practice, the effect of this concession was felt most strongly in France and Italy, where duties at the start were generally considerably higher than in Benelux and Germany.) The second reduction by ten per cent was duly put into operation on July 1, 1960, by a simple repetition of the cut 'across the board' in all rates and without recourse to the more complex Treaty provisions.

The carrying out of the agreements on quotas was expected to be particularly difficult for France, where imports remained strictly controlled until the radical change in economic policy at the end of 1958 which brought France into line with its partners. By far the most troublesome problems arose in connection with the 'three per cent rule' on goods for which quotas had previously been very small or non-existent. 'National output' was a vague term and if it was interpreted in terms of value, the effect of devaluation on prices could make a big difference. The Commission had a good deal of difficulty in ensuring the application of the Treaty, particularly during the first half of 1959. In some cases the delays seem to have prevented importers from filling the theoretically available quotas, and France and Italy were particularly adept at this game. A year later, at the beginning of 1960, conditions were much more favourable and in each case more than the minimum rise of one-fifth was achieved. A third increase in quotas was smoothly put into effect on January 1, 1961.

Although the Commission did not find the reduction in quantitative restrictions quite such plain sailing as the cut in duties, most disputes could be settled by agreement with the national governments, but the Commission had to sue Germany and Italy before the Court of Justice, because they refused to comply with the directives on imports of certain meat products. On December 21, 1961, the Court ruled against Italy and in favour of the Commission. (In April, 1961, the Commission made another successful complaint to the Court about Italian duty rates on radio tubes and valves and in February, 1962, against Belgium-Luxembourg about import fees on honey cake.)

With these minor exceptions, the practice of the Community in respect of 'economic disarmament' was thus fully in line with the terms of the Treaty. However, new conditions called for even faster action. The prosperity of most of the Member States was exceeding the most sanguine expectations and invited further progress, while the growing outside pressure from Britain and other European countries increased the need for it. The last factor was undoubtedly more important, and the Commission came to the conclusion 'that Europe must be made and, to be made, must be made quickly'.[2] This was the basis of the so-called acceleration policy.

The Politics of Acceleration

The proposal was to speed up the removal of trade barriers within the Community at a faster pace than provided for by the Treaty. This plan was first mooted by the Commission in the summer of 1959 and brought before the Council in October by the Belgian Foreign Minister, M. Wigny. The Commission was then instructed to formulate specific proposals and this process went on against the background of intense negotiations between the Member States. Final recommendations were submitted to the Council in February, 1960, the European Parliament was informed in March and the Council's decision was reached on May 12, 1960.

The issue which had to be resolved before this result was achieved was a twin conflict of interests between the high-tariff countries France and Italy and the rest and between industrialists and farmers everywhere. The first took the form of negotiations around the early introduction of the common external tariff which was demanded mainly by France. According to the Treaty, the first step towards the common tariff should be made at the same time as the reduction of thirty per cent in duties on intra-Community trade. It was now proposed to reach this point after three years instead of four and France claimed with impeccable logic that the link between the two processes should be retained and that the low-tariff countries should raise their rates against third countries, as otherwise there would be a serious danger of 'distortion of trade'.

The other side of the medal was the uneven distribution of gains and losses between industrial and agricultural interests. The obstacles to agricultural trade were largely independent of tariff levels and should be overcome by the introduction of a common policy. Although the two years originally allotted for

[2] *Third General Report*, para. 4.

this task were over, the recently published first draft of the Commission's proposals was a long way removed from the acceptance of a common agricultural policy, and the outstanding importer, W. Germany, was dragging its feet about admitting more agricultural imports from its partners at the expense of its trade relations with the outside world. France, Italy and the Netherlands, therefore, demanded a definite commitment in the agricultural sphere in the form of an agreed time table for the adoption of a common policy.

These clashes of interests between the Member States were overshadowed by the political implications of the rivalry between the Six and the Outer Seven under British leadership. French insistence that the low-tariff countries should make a start with increasing their duties against third countries and actively 'discriminate' in favour of the Community members was specifically intended to prevent agreement between the Six and the Seven on terms which would have weakened the EEC. The ingenious solution finally adopted was proposed by the Commission. It was agreed that the first step towards the common external tariff should be taken, but for this purpose its level would be provisionally reduced by twenty per cent: 'This twenty per cent represents an advance suspension of duties pending the results of the tariff negotiations in GATT which will make it possible to judge whether the conditions of reciprocity offered by non-member States are satisfactory . . .'[3]

The great diplomatic merit of this proposal was its dual-purpose character: it was ostensibly held out as a carrot to third countries, above all to the United States and Britain, which were offered a liberal tariff policy in exchange for equivalent concessions; but it could be used as a stick, if the other GATT members continued with their embarrassing attacks on the Rome Treaty. (In its final form, the concession was not applied automatically to the 'particularly sensitive' products on List G and limited to duties which would not thereby be reduced below the agreed common external tariff.[4] In addition there was a special dispensation for Germany concerning duties which had been reduced in August, 1957, to meet the economic situation.)

Simultaneously with the partial alignment of duties vis-à-vis third countries, duties on industrial products traded between Member States were cut by an additional ten per cent on De-

[3] *Third General Report*, para. 10.   [4] *ibid*, para. 15.

cember 31, 1960, bringing the total to thirty per cent. A further ten per cent cut was due according to the terms of the Treaty at the end of 1961, and it was agreed that, in addition, the Council would decide by mid-1961 in the light of general economic conditions whether this could be doubled. Thus all duties on industrial goods in trade between the Six would have been halved in the space of four years. Finally it was agreed that all quantitative restrictions on intra-Community trade in non-agricultural goods should be totally abolished by the end of 1961.

These sweeping proposals were applied to agriculture only very partially. Agricultural products were excluded from the move towards the common external tariff and the acceleration was limited to five per cent for 'non-liberalized' commodities— without the second reduction provisionally envisaged for industrial products. The decision which really mattered in this field—at least at the time—was the specific promise 'that the measures provided for in the Treaty, but not yet implemented, must be put into effect before December 31, 1960'.[5] For this purpose the Council laid down a detailed (but wholly illusory) time table with the proviso that adequate progress had to be made in this field by the end of the year, before the acceleration plan as a whole could be put into effect; it will be shown later on how the mounting dissatisfaction with Germany's lack of co-operation in the promised common agricultural policy in the end delayed the achievement of the second stage of the acceleration plan and endangered the transition from the first stage to the second stage of the Common Market as a whole.

However, on May 12, 1960, this cloud on the horizon was no bigger than Dr Erhard's hand and, to round off the process of mutual re-assurance, the Council adopted a solemn 'declaration of intent' which echoed earlier demands of the European Parliament for the acceleration of integration in all sectors covered by the Treaty, and particularly in the social field.

This important complex of negotiations and decisions reflects the characteristic mode of operation of the Six. The drive towards the creation of a large trading area unhampered by internal restrictions is spear-headed by the predominant industrial interests. They more than maintain the initiative which has always been theirs from the very inception of the Community,

[5] ibid., para. 18.

but they are not in a position to use sledge-hammer tactics and have to cajole the other interests and to make promises of future good behaviour in order to get their way immediately.

At the same time they are tough bargainers who do not err on the side of generosity—witness the German claim to have done their duty by their partners for the first two duty reductions and a half by their unilateral tariff cut in August, 1957, and their success in limiting duty increases against third countries at the end of 1960 to half of the reductions made on that occasion. In fact, the growing strength of Germany within the Six caused the German negotiators to overplay their hand; this was not very much in evidence during 1960, though the discussions preceding the final decision in December were long and at times acrimonious, and the Council finally agreed to put the first part of the acceleration programme into effect according to plan.

The decision about the second leg of the programme was due to be made by the end of June, 1961, six months before it was to be moved to the agreed position. Although the Commission advised the Council in good time that economic conditions favoured such a step, the attempt to keep up the pressure on 'industrial disarmament' irrespective of progress in other fields of the economy was strongly resisted by France, Italy and the Netherlands, all of which were by now convinced that Germany had no intention of keeping its side of the bargain without being compelled to do so. Germany was, indeed, arguing that the acceleration decision had already been taken and that progress was, therefore, automatic provided economic conditions were favourable, which could not be denied; the other side was adamant in its demand 'that precise targets, to be attained in the near future should be fixed in the field of social, agricultural and transport policy, and the speed-up measures in the field of tariffs examined in the same context as these targets.'[6]

The unevenness in carrying the Treaty into effect was thus even greater than the unequal balance in the terms of the Treaty itself. In practice this lack of balance was intensified by the inherent conflict of interests between Germany and the other partners (except Belgium) and by Germany's steadily growing reluctance to make concessions which its increasing bargaining power seemed to make unnecessary. As a result of the ensuing

[6] *Bulletin*, June, 1961, p. 33.

deadlock, the Council was unable to endorse the further acceleration measures by the end of June, 1961, and had to put them off to the end of the year. For the rest of 1961, things moved steadily towards the showdown of the marathon December negotiations in the Council which led to a first-rate crisis within the Community and endangered the progress to the second stage of the Common Market. Thus bigger issues were at stake than an additional ten per cent cut in industrial duties which therefore had to be put off for six months.

Capital Transfers

By overreaching themselves, partly under the influence of home political considerations, the Germans thus rendered a disservice to the interests of big business and demonstrated the limits of its power within the EEC. The reality of this power is nevertheless a fundamental fact for the Community, and it was strikingly illustrated by the degree of priority accorded to the freeing of capital movements.

In this important respect, 'acceleration', though completely unheralded and achieved without any great difficulty, far exceeded the provisions of art. 67 of the Treaty which says only that 'Member States shall, in the course of the transitional period and to the extent necessary for the proper functioning of the Common Market, progressively abolish as between themselves restrictions on the movement of capital belonging to persons resident in Member States . . .' The only step foreseen by the Treaty by the end of the first stage was the liberalization of current payments connected with movements of capital between the Six. The same caution was evident in the rules of procedure on the subject which included unanimity in the Council during the first two transitional stages.

In fact the Commission, with the support of the Monetary Committee, set to work on this problem during the Community's initial year of operations. Both were agreed 'on the necessity for the widest and most rapid liberalization possible, so that the other measures of liberalization provided for in the Treaty concerning goods, services and persons and the right of establishment might have their full effect.'[7] The key position thus attributed to capital movements by the Commission, but not by the treaty, may owe something to external developments,

[7] *Third General Report*, para. 128f.

such as the pressure for currency convertibility in 1958. It was accepted that the liberalization of capital transfers 'could upset the balance of payments of the States concerned or that they might not be channelled in an economically desirable direction' —at least 'so long as economic, monetary and financial policies have not been sufficiently co-ordinated'. This calculated risk was taken and the Commission intentionally concentrated on the liberalization of capital movements as the most effective way of ensuring the co-ordination of the broad economic policies of the Member States on lines meeting with the approval of the owners of large financial resources (though not, at this stage, of short-term speculators).

The first Council direction on the liberalization of capital movements was issued in May, 1960, and entered into force in the following month. It contained a substantial advance towards the goal of complete freedom of important types of capital transfers and correspondingly limited the powers of the Member States to use exchange control as an instrument of economic policy.

The directive decreed the unconditional liberalization of direct investments within the Community as well as that of personal capital movements connected with short-term or medium-term commercial transactions and dealings in securities quoted on stock exchanges, though these may be temporarily limited to finance houses and certain types of firms (Art. I and II). At the same time, conditional liberalization (which may be suspended in case of need by member governments in consultation with the Commission) was accorded to capital market issues, medium-term and long-term loans, financial credits and dealings in unquoted securities (Art. III), while short-term capital movements with their dangerous speculative possibilities were for the time being excluded from liberalization.

The most important effect of this regulation was the consolidation of a number of monetary measures taken by individual governments since the return to convertibility, thus subjecting them 'to rules which cannot be unilaterally annulled except by applying a fixed procedure'.[8] This virtual elimination of exchange control as a method of insulating the domestic economy against outside pressure might well have the effect in times of emergency to narrow down the alternatives open to a

[8] Third General Report, para. 131.

country to the stark choice between deflation and devaluation.

The directive had little practical significance for Germany and Belgium-Luxembourg, where currency transactions were already substantially unrestricted. The unconditional liberalization measures covered by art. I and II of the directive were duly put into operation by each Member State, but France, Italy and the Netherlands availed themselves of the escape clause for conditionally liberalized transactions under art. III.

The next step envisaged by the Commission is a regulation freeing invisible transactions not connected with the movement of goods, services, capital and persons, an exhaustive list of which is given in the third Appendix to the Treaty. Its text provides only that for the time being there should be a standstill on transfer restrictions on these items (art. 106) and that the programme for abolishing them should be agreed before the end of the first stage (art. 63). The favourable economic conditions of the last few years should make it possible to improve in practice on this time table.

Commercial and Economic Policy

Only moderate progress was made in the first stage with the creation of a common commercial policy towards third countries which is to be worked out during the transitional period. Trade agreements between Member States and third countries are liable to affect the preferential position of the other partners, particularly in agricultural trade where bilateral agreements continue to play an important part. This is, again, largely a German problem, for Germany continues to make good use of its position as an importer of primary commodities to safeguard its exports of industrial goods to third markets. It is only natural that this should have given rise to demands that the scope of such agreements should be limited to prevent their interference with the progress of the Common Market.

In response to this pressure the Commission submitted to the Council in the summer of 1961 certain proposals for the coordination of the external trade policy of the Member States during the period of transition. These proposals were part of the campaign of the agricultural exporters within the Community for better treatment by Germany, and their adoption by the Council was a preliminary success for the advocates of an active common agricultural policy.

The decisions which the Council made in October, 1961, concern two important matters of procedure; both should tie the hands of governments using bilateral trade agreements in order to continue to get the best of both worlds. The first instructed the Member States to inform each other (and the Commission) each quarter of all important trade negotiations pending during the next three months, and to consult them in advance; the second prohibited all bilateral trade agreements terminating after the end of the period of transition, limited certain types of agreements to a period of one year and empowered the Commission to scrutinize all such agreements before the end of 1965 in order to ensure that they could not form an obstacle to the introduction of a common commercial policy.

In the field of general economic policy the Treaty of Rome limited itself to the platitude that Member States should consider 'their policy relating to economic trends as a matter of common interest' (art. 103(1)) and that they should consult each other and the Commission in case of need. The rapid advance towards full currency convertibility in 1959 and the possible incompatibility of monetary measures taken by one Member State with the interests of another were amongst the reasons for setting up the Committee on Economic Trends and of a special working party on employment trends in different parts of the Community.

Though there has been some progress in the co-ordination of financial policy, the most important event of 1961 in this field, the revaluation of the Deutsche Mark, did not produce much evidence of its effectiveness. It was apparently decided on by the German government on its own initiative and took the other Member States completely by surprise—including the Dutch who hurriedly fell into line within twenty-four hours, because they could not afford the consequences of a fall in the value of the guilder compared with the Deutsche Mark in the prevailing boom conditions.

The Commission kept up appearances by welcoming both decisions, but the episode shows the extreme difficulties of effectively harmonizing general economic policies between Member States whose economic systems continue to develop at very uneven rates and far from harmoniously. Despite the frequent meetings of the Ministers of Finance of the Six, their attitude at the important meeting of the International Monetary

Fund in Vienna (September, 1961) also showed substantial differences between the German view and that of the French and Dutch delegations.

(3) COMPETITION

The Rules of the Game

Apart from differences in exchange rates and the level of the external tariffs of the Member States, the competitive conditions of producers in different countries may be affected by a host of national arrangements. These include, in particular, State aids to their own nationals in the awarding of public contracts, export assistance through financial inducements and special taxation devices. In addition, the co-existence of half a dozen different legal and administrative systems forms an obstacle to the free flow of goods, even where there is no conscious intention of distorting competitive conditions to the detriment of the foreigner.

The European Commission has been busy on the unification of competitive conditions in all these fields; its success so far has been far from negligible, though it has barely touched the fringe of the problem. The most straightforward issues arise in connection with dumping practices, where the Commission has a definite mandate under the Treaty. Its action has taken two main forms; in March, 1960, and April, 1961, it made two regulations under the 'boomerang clause' (art. 91(2)) which permits the recipient of intra-Community imports to re-export them to the sending country free of duty; in addition, it has investigated a number of specific complaints from governments and firms and has acted as honest broker between the contestants. As a rule, this resulted in the termination of the objectionable practices, and by the middle of April, 1961, formal recommendations had been issued in respect of only two enterprises.

State aids in general presented a much more complex problem; unlike dumping they were not unconditionally outlawed by the Treaty but permitted in cases where they do not involve national discrimination or where they relate to regional development, to projects of European significance or to conditions of serious economic disturbance (art. 92). These exceptions are of special importance for France and Italy which employ a whole host of measures including 'credit facilities, guarantees, capital subsidies and tax advantages',[9] while support for the ship-building industry is common to a number of countries. (The same applies to some features of the Belgian *Loi Unique* and to Germany's support for the synthetic rubber industry.)

Action by the Commission comes up against the virtual impossibility of deciding whether broad enabling laws fall under the general prohibition of State aids or the permitted exceptions. It has been claimed that the Commission should have the right of sitting in judgment on specific administrative measures under such laws, but its power to do this under art. 93 of the Treaty is far from clear.

A problem of particularly great practical importance is that of export drawbacks and import levies arising from the turnover tax systems in force in all the Member States. A number of working parties and study groups have been set up on the subject of harmonizing national systems or replacing them by a single set of rules for the Community as a whole which may be the only way out. Meanwhile the Council decided in June, 1960, to 'freeze' existing rates as an interim measure. Certain increases made on various occasions by the Netherlands and by the Belgian *Loi Unique* were accepted as justified, but long and intricate negotiations arose from the Italian decision in September, 1960, to increase rates on 800 customs items. A compromise was reached in May, 1961, which accepted Italy's action where export drawbacks and import levies did not exceed five per cent, but scaled down to some extent rates above this level.

There is as yet little to show for the enormous amount of work done on the approximation of legal and administrative systems which affect trade between the member countries, but plans have been worked out for a European system of pattern and trade marks, a non-discriminatory code of practice for public contracts, etc.

Anti-Cartel Regulations

In the Treaty of Rome, and in the administrative practice of the Commission, the protection of producers from unfair handicaps through the action of national governments is combined with the protection of consumers from restrictive practices by

[9] *Fourth General Report*, para. 57.

producers. However, these tasks are essentially very different
and affect important interests in very different ways. Always
excepting the immediate beneficiaries, all groups of producers
are normally in favour of rules of the game which keep the
scales even between them; on the other hand, different sections
of the business classes disagree profoundly about the merits of
legally enforced competition between enterprises, while most
other sections of the population are enthusiastically in favour
of stringent anti-cartel legislation.

The theoretical hostility of the Treaty of Rome towards
cartels, monopolies and other restrictive devices stems from two
different sources—the heritage of the ECSC and the principles
of the 'social market economy'. It is difficult, and not a little
ironical, to remember in 1962 the resolute opposition of the
Western powers to the rebirth of German monopoly capitalism
as a whole, and particularly in the heavy industry of the Ruhr.
In the years immediately following the German surrender, there
was an almost universal conviction that 'deconcentration' was
the necessary condition for avoiding the political peril of
German economic domination over Europe. (Nor is there any
good reason to disagree with this judgment even now; the mis-
take, such as it was, consisted in regarding the break-up of the
German economic empire as a sufficient as well as a necessary
condition of a healthier balance of power in Europe.)

This attitude is reflected in the 'supra-national' powers of the
High Authority of the ECSC and in the stringency of the anti-
cartel and anti-monopoly paragraphs of the Treaty by which
it was set up. The interminable and not very effective attempts
of the Authority to reconcile the factual cartelization of the
German coal industry and the re-growth of huge steel empires
with the plain terms of the Treaty indicate its fading con-
victions or, at the very least, its impotence in the face of
Germany's re-assertion of economic leadership.

While based on the experience of its older sister, the anti-
cartel and anti-monopoly legislation of the EEC also reflects
the firm belief of the founding fathers of the Community in the
virtue of free competition as a spur to economic efficiency and
as a safeguard to the public against the anti-social exploitation
of the new opportunities which the Common Market provided
for the business classes. The model of an allegedly successful
practical application of such a policy was Western Germany

and its most prominent apostle the loquacious guardian of the German economic miracle, Professor Ludwig Erhard, the Minister of Economics and permanent heir apparent to Dr Adenauer. In his own words, 'in a discussion of cartel policy we are not dealing with just one of many points at issue. Here we are dealing above all with the central problem of our economic order.'[10]

Articles 85 and 86 of the Treaty of Rome do not fully express this strong and naïve conviction, but in the hands of a determined and independent authority they might well assume considerable importance. Their weakness does not lie in their admirably defined intentions, which are excellent, but in the sweeping qualifications by which they may easily be frustrated in practice. At first sight nothing could be plainer than the outlawing of all cartels and similar agreements 'likely to affect trade between the Member States and which have as their object or result the prevention, restriction or distortion of competition within the Common Market'. (art. 85(1)); a net drawn so wide should surely catch all but the smallest fry.

However, despite its loud roar the lion of competition is at bottom only Bottom the weaver. The third section of article 85 exempts cartels from this blanket prohibition, if they 'contribute to the improvement of the production or distribution of goods or to the promotion of technical or economic progress while reserving to users an equitable share in the profit resulting therefrom.' This is very different from the gaunt requirement concerning the public interest used by the British Restrictive Trade Practices Act, and it should not be beyond the resources of the legal profession to claim the benefit of one or the other of these saving clauses. Similarly, though art. 86 is better than nothing (which is by and large the British position), it does not prohibit monopolies but is confined to *actions* taking 'improper advantage of a dominant position within the Common Market', and even then only 'to the extent to which trade between the Member States may be affected thereby'.

The same push and pull of discordant interests can be traced in the ambiguous time table for putting these rules into effect. The opening statement is, again, clear enough, for it instructs the Council to adopt by a unanimous vote the appropriate regulations and directives applying these principles 'within a period

[10] *Prosperity through Competition* (English translation 1958), p. 129.

C

of three years after the entry into force of this Treaty' (art. 87). However, this does not make it mandatory for the Council to do so, it only means that otherwise they may be adopted by the Council on a qualified majority, without any further time limit. In the meantime, the national governments are charged with the application of these principles, though the Commission may make investigations and publish their results.

There is now, as there has been since the creation of the ECSC, a clear division of labour between the apostles of free competition within a social market economy and the facts of European economic life: the former write the Treaties and the latter tacitly re-assert themselves in their operation. The recent history of the Commission's attempts to put art. 85 and 86 into operation is merely another illustration of this fact.

The Commission's action was heralded in July, 1960, by M. Jean Monnet's influential Action Committee which made no bones about the current situation: 'The firm application of a European anti-trust law is essential in order that all consumers and producers alike enjoy the benefits of a vast single market. The large number of agreements and concentrations envisaged or concluded as part of the producers' reaction to the Common Market underline the risk that it will be dominated and divided by monopolies and cartels.'[11] The first draft regulation on this subject was finally transmitted to the Council at the end of October, 1960—only two months before the end of the time limit for a unanimous decision, and the reference of the proposals to the Economic and Social Council and to the European Parliament prevented adherence to the dead line, for the Economic Council gave its opinion in March, 1961, while the European Parliament discussed it in October of the same year.

Though mainly concerned with procedure, the Commission's proposals aroused bitter opposition, because they might have become a serious challenge to deep-seated industrial mores. All agreements covered by the basic condemnation of art. 85(1) were to be outlawed forthwith, unless they had been specifically exempted by the Commission at the request of the parties concerned. It was, therefore, proposed that all agreements brought to the notice of the Commission should be allowed to continue provisionally, unless the Commission objected to them, within six months in the case of new agreements. Exemptions would

---

[11] Quoted by E. Benoit, *Europe at Sixes and Sevens* (New York 1961), p. 44.

be granted for a limited period, rather than permanently, though with provision for their extension, and the decision on exemptions was to be entirely in the hands of the Commission, thus removing this crucial power entirely from the national authorities. Last but not least, obligatory notification was to apply to certain especially important categories of cartels which could be particularly harmful to the Common Market, and the Commission could impose fines of $100-5,000 for withholding information and penalties of $50-1,000 per day in case of delay in registrations; though not unreasonable, these amounts were sufficiently high to compel firms to take the legislation seriously.

The discussion in the Economic and Social Committee showed an open cleavage on the registration of existing agreements. The cartelization of wide areas of the economy in the Community is a well-established fact which has not been altered by the enactment of anti-cartel laws in most of the Member States. The application of the Community's anti-cartel laws by a Commission misguided enough to take a serious view of the tenets of the social market economy could be a serious nuisance to the dominant interests if it were extended to existing arrangements, but it would be a harmless mockery if confined to future agreements. On this issue the Committee split right down the middle, with forty-one in favour of compulsory registration, forty-one against and ten abstentions, with all the workers' representatives in favour and all the employers against compulsory declaration.[12]

In the Council the opposition to the Commission's plan was apparently led by France and Italy, and the draft was substantially modified before agreement could be reached at the end of December, 1961, just four years after the start of the EEC. The compromise is on lines much more acceptable to the business community than the original proposals. Certain types of existing agreements are specifically exempted from registration and the Commission must exercise its powers in close co-operation with the national authorities under the virtual supervision of a consultative committee representing them and, therefore, much less independently of the interests affected by its actions. The only serious clash of views between the Community and the dominant business interests has thus entailed one of the few major checks to the Commission and resulted in a compromise

[12] *Bulletin*, April, 1961, p. 45.

whose effects on the *status quo* cannot yet be foreseen.

Early in 1961 the Commission published a volume of over 500 pages devoted entirely to the listing of trade associations on the Community level—a veritable directory of vested interests in the Six. There were fifty-four organizations representing industry (excluding the food industries which are closely related to agriculture), twenty-two commercial organizations (excluding trade in agricultural products) and six organizations covering small business either on its own or in connection with industry and trade—a total of eighty-two bodies on the Community level, apart from the Standing Committee of the Chambers of Commerce of the Six and a special committee of the Union of International Fairs. As it would be impracticable to consult on every occasion with such numbers, industry, commerce and handicrafts each have their 'central organization authorized to watch over the general interests of their members';[13] these are the influential spokesmen of their respective groups in direct contact with the official bodies of the Community.

The corresponding agricultural organizations happened to have exactly the same number in December, 1960—they were in all eighty-two bodies, comprising '9 farmers' organizations, 6 organizations of agricultural co-operatives, 36 organizations in the agricultural and foodstuffs industries, 27 organizations in the field of trade in agricultural produce and foodstuffs, 3 organizations of workers in the agricultural and foodstuffs sector and 1 consumers' organization (consumers co-operatives)'. As with trade and industry, there are roof organizations grouping these bodies into four main interests.

As the Monet Committee noticed, the first four years of the EEC have been a time of amazing growth in lateral and vertical links amongst business firms which paralleled or exceeded the spawning of trade associations on a Community basis. Mergers and take-overs were (and continue to be) announced in the trade press almost daily, supplemented by specialization agreements between previously competing firms and marketing agreements between competitors which virtually exclude effective competition, because they frequently share out the marketing of competing products.

Faced with this avalanche of actually or potentially anti-com-

13 *Bulletin,* April, 1961, pp. 11ff.

petitive activities by business firms intent on adapting the structure of the Community to their profit interests, the Commission reached the plaintive conclusion that, however remarkable these events as evidence of the unbounded confidence of industry in the future of the Community, 'it may also be thought that in some cases these forms of co-operation call for examination under the rules of competition'.[14]

This massive understatement contrasts strongly with the Commission's usual flair for the telling phrase and the art of the public relations officer; similarly, the practical conclusion of intending to keep this development under consideration compares unfavourably with the incisive action of which it has proved capable on occasions where it was in full agreement with big business interests rather than in potential opposition to them.

(4) ESTABLISHMENT, SERVICES AND TRANSPORT

Freeing Establishment and the Supply of Services
The 'right of establishment' has two separate aspects, one personal and one commercial. In the personal sense it implies the right of setting up in any member country in a trade or profession; commercially it means the right of companies to set up branch organizations throughout the Community and its associated territories. In both respects the Treaty decrees the abolition of national discrimination in the course of the period of transition (art. 53), but its time table is fairly exacting, for the Commission is instructed to submit within two years a general programme for the abolition of such discrimination and the Council must adopt such a programme by the end of the first stage (art. 54(1)); its general principles are elaborated in considerable detail in the Treaty itself. An exactly parallel procedure is laid down for the liberalization of services supplied for remuneration (art. 63), and the two subjects are closely linked.

The Commission's first step was the drawing up of directives for enabling nationals of all Member States to establish themselves in the associated overseas territories. This plan was worked out in 1958, and in the early part of 1960 this was

14 *Fourth General Report*, para. 70.

followed by general programmes on the right of establishment and the supply of services. The drafts were referred by the Council to the Economic and Social Committee in May and September, 1960, respectively and returned with the Committee's general blessing in February, 1961. After a discussion in the European Parliament in March the programmes were endorsed by the Council in October, 1961.

The programme in its final form is very flexible and lays down only maximum periods. The first step will be taken by the end of 1963 with the removal of national discrimination for most industrial and commercial activities with special safeguards for handicrafts whose protection is important for social and political reasons. Longer delays are foreseen for the food industries, insurance and retail trade and some of the liberal professions (end of the second stage), transport, life insurance—which are to be liberalized by the end of the second year of stage three —and agriculture; 'inelastic' industries such as shipbuilding, railway equipment, aircraft construction and forestry will have to wait until the end of the transitional period.

'The time table drawn up in the light of similar considerations for the two programmes, i.e. essentially the priority of liberalization of activities which are particularly beneficial for the development of production and trade, is practically the same for establishment and services, though the pace is more rapid in the case of the latter.'[15]

Transport

At first sight there would seem to be insufficient reason to single out transport for special treatment from other service industries, at least to the extent of reserving a full Department of the Commission for its supervision, but in fact it has presented the Treaty makers with difficult problems which still await an adequate solution. The pre-Treaty negotiations failed to arrive at detailed agreements between the parties, and the eleven articles of the Treaty of Rome devoted to the subject (74-84) are amongst its vaguest and most heavily qualified sections. They barely touch the content of the postulated 'common transport policy' and find the greatest difficulty in reconciling the principle of uniform and non-discriminatory tariffs with the fact that concessionary transport rates are one

[15] *Fourth General Report*, para. 42.

of the most frequently used forms of protection and subsidization of tender interests.

The glaring omission of air and sea transport, though perhaps intended to reduce the area of disagreement, must hamstring the Community in any attempt to plan a rational transport system for the Six. The importance of transport for the Common Market lies, indeed, in two fields—the need for a modern and efficient transport network ensuring the smooth flow of persons and goods and the possibility of substantial distortions of trade through discriminatory transport rates. Of these, the second is relatively by far the easier issue, and the Treaty articles devoted to this problem are much more specific than the rest. They prescribe action directed against discrimination on grounds of nationality between carriers and in transport rates during the first two years of the Community's existence and demand that 'rates and conditions involving any element of support or protection' (art. 80(1)) are to disappear at the end of the first stage, though this may well be frustrated by the proviso that this prohibition 'shall not apply to competitive tariffs' (art. 80(3)).

Regulation 11 has made a beginning with putting these provisions into effect with rules for ending national discrimination in transport rates and conditions and for an internal transport document which finally entered into force in September, 1960, though the Member States were given until the end of June, 1961, for the institution of the necessary controls.

Tentative time tables for future progress propose that by 1964 carriers from other Member States shall be able to engage in domestic transport at the beginning and end of international runs, while all forms of national discrimination on domestic transport shall cease by the end of 1967.

With the quickening pace of integration, the common transport policy assumed increasing urgency, and in April, 1961, the Commission published its ideas on the subject. These seem to have had a mixed reception by the Council in June, though the Permanent Representatives accepted the Memorandum as a basis for further studies in the light of the Council's debate.

The document provided little more than a framework for future efforts. In a field where technical developments and economic needs would seem to cry out for a bold overall policy, the Memorandum's starting point was the general lack of free competition in transport which it attributed to the existence of 'special features', such as the financing of infra-structure expenditure on roads and waterways from public funds, the special burden on the railways as common carriers, etc.

Dominated by the idea of making transport as competitive as possible, the draft does not regard this as evidence of the need for a different approach but as simple nuisances which 'can be eliminated in part or mitigated . . . and thus the disturbances which they cause on the transport market remedied'.[16] Thus the Commission proposed the introduction of the greatest possible degree of competition between different forms of transport, though this would require an equitable distribution of infra-structure costs, a reorganization of the railways and the relaxation of their obligations as common carriers. On this basis five 'guiding principles' are formulated:

'(i) Equality of treatment between enterprises and means of transport on the one hand and users on the other;
(ii) Financial autonomy of enterprises;
(iii) Freedom of action for the enterprises in fixing rates and in access to the various transport markets;
(iv) Free choice for the users, which implies the freedom of transport on own account under certain conditions;
(v) Co-ordination of investments in the light of European economic integration.'[17]

No fundamental changes were proposed in the system of fixed rates for scheduled passenger services, but for goods traffic the Commission envisaged the 'progressive establishment of a system of rate brackets coupled with checks and a certain form of publicity'.[18] Hauliers would thus be free to quote rates 'within limits chosen to avoid excessive competition or monopoly. Only the limits of the bracket will have to be made public in advance'. These extremely laboured and artificial proposals reflect the Commission's caution after the failure—reputedly as a result of Dutch resistance—of its earlier attempt to secure compulsory publication of rates; this compromise is comparable with the watering down of the Commission's anti-cartel regulations as a result of Italo-French resistance.

[16] *Bulletin*, July-August, 1961, p. 39.
[17] *ibid.*, p. 41.   [18] *ibid.*, p. 42.

This attempt to steer a common policy between divergent national and sectional interests is no less problematical than the Commission's overall approach to an industry where its whole economic philosophy may prove in practice either irrelevant or harmful. However, detailed criticism would be premature, as the final policy may well differ substantially from the Commission's plans for which at the moment not even a detailed timetable has been laid down. Tentative dates have been fixed for the introduction of very modest preliminary rules for international goods transport by road.

(5) LABOUR

The Treaty wished to establish a completely free labour market within the Community by the end of the transitional period with prohibition of national discrimination 'as regards employment, remuneration and other working conditions' (art. 48(2)), though these rights are conditional on 'offers of employment actually made' which would seem to prevent nationals of one Member State from looking for work in the territory of another, unless already resident there. The timetable for giving effect to these aims directed the Council to take the necessary measures (on a proposal by the Commission) 'upon the entry into force of this Treaty' (art. 49); taken literally, this would have involved almost absolute priority for this task. Art. 51 also instructs the Council to ensure that workers' social security contributions and benefits are made fully transferable within the Community.

In practice, the partial introduction of the free movement of labour proved far from easy, and despite the energy of the Commission it has taken much longer to make tangible progress with it than with the liberalization of capital transfers. The Commission's first (1959) draft was amended following consultations with government experts, trade unions and employers' associations, and it was not until July, 1960, that the proposed regulation and directive were submitted to the Council. Although the Treaty does not expressly provide for this, the European Parliament was consulted in October and the Economic and Social Committee reported on the drafts in November, 1960. Following further amendments and negotiations the Council finally adopted the measure in August, 1961, and it entered into force one month later, almost four years after the Treaty itself.

For the creation of a free labour market, the rights of immigrants must be reconciled with the claims of the indigenous workers for the maintenance of their jobs and living standards. As the Great Boom of 1959-61 virtually eliminated unemployment in five out of the six Member States, conditions could hardly have been more favourable for the new policy. It was, indeed, possible to claim as one of its results 'the possibility of reducing the working week to a normal length so that the practice of working overtime, which is becoming more and more frequent in countries suffering from grave manpower shortages, will become less widespread'.[19]

The measure has two parts—a 'directive' to the member governments which deals with the administrative aspects of migrant labour control, and a 'regulation' which establishes a new law for the whole Community. This Regulation 15 has four main parts. Part I regulates the rights of immigrant workers and their families. It allows the Labour Exchanges of each Member State three weeks for filling existing vacancies with their own nationals, unless an employer specifically names a worker from another Community country. After this time limit the job is open throughout the Six.

After working in another country for twelve months, an immigrant has a right to the renewal of his labour permit in the same occupation; after three years he may claim a permit for any job for which he is qualified, and after four years' work in his new country his rights are the same as those of native workers. As the right of settlement would be a mockery if it excluded the worker's family, full provision is made for admitting his spouse and family to the host country.

In order to operate these provisions, Part II sets up a complex system of notification of vacancies. For this purpose a European Office for the co-ordinatioon and clearing of vacancies and applications for employment is envisaged. Part III contains details of the consultative and technical committees with tripartite representation, which are to assist the Commission in running the new system, while the most important provision of Part IV is art. 43 which enjoins Member States to give priority

[19] L. Levi Sandri, *The free movement of workers in the countries of the EEC*, Bulletin, June, 1961, p. 9.

to qualified unemployed workers of another Member State in filling general vacancies—a form of preference which might confront the United Kingdom with an all but insoluble political dilemma.

In a Community where more than one million people are working outside their country of origin, the protection of the rights of migrant workers to social security is no negligible matter. This problem has employed a special administrative committee almost monthly for more than three years, apart from numerous meetings between the experts of the Commission, the national governments, trade unions and employers' organizations. The purely technical difficulties of dealing with six different national legislations in four languages are formidable, and the dividing line between measures relating primarily to the free movement of workers and those forming part of the Community's social policy is somewhat artificial.

Social Policy

The Treaty of Rome devoted considerable attention to the creation of a common social policy. It staked a claim to being a socially progressive document by insisting on 'the necessity to promote improvement of the living and working conditions of labour so as to permit the equalization of such conditions in an upward direction' (art. 117), but its practical emphasis was mainly on two aspects with a direct bearing on its economic aims. These are the social changes needed to make labour fully mobile, including the setting up of a European Social Fund (art. 123-8), and the prevention of trade distortion as a result of strong national differences in social legislation (art. 119-20).

In practice, the Commission soon came to the conclusion that 'the first aim of any co-ordination of social policies at the present time must be the optimum utilization of the human resources of the Community'[20] and that the best way of reaching it was the concentration of effort on improving the occupational mobility of labour and, above all, on smoothing the flow of workers from agriculture to industry. As this 'common policy of occupational training must necessarily be considered the linch pin of the Commission's future action in the social field',[21] it was naturally the main interest of the European Social Fund envisaged by the Treaty and the subject of a draft order tabled late in 1961.

[20] Third General Report, para. 283.   [21] ibid., para. 289.

The drafting, discussion and amendment of its Statute proved to be a lengthy job, but it was finally set up in the autumn of 1960 and began work in the following year. The Fund first figured in the Budget of the Community for 1959 with 500m. B. Francs (about £3½m.); this sum was carried forward to the next budget, when a similar amount was voted. The budget for 1961 contained a credit of 1,000m. B. Francs for this purpose which was increased by an unspent balance of 500m. B. Francs from 1960, giving it a total working capital of almost £11m. at the end of 1961. As its task is to finance one-half of the expenditure incurred by public authorities for the occupational retraining of unemployed workers (but not of 'independent' peasants), for the resettlement of unemployed workers and the maintenance of the wage level of workers affected by the conversion of 'their' enterprises to other uses, the total amount available for these purposes up to the end of the financial year 1961 was almost £22m.

The equalization of social legislation and security involves short-term as well as long-term issues. Looking towards the future, the Commission has initiated an impressive number of studies and investigations in the field of employment and social security which may one day make a very useful contribution towards planned progress in this field on a European basis. For the present, the most urgent technical problems have arisen in connection with the social insurance of migrant workers whose flow increased steeply with the advance of the economic boom, while the most important economic issues arose from the agreements for the harmonization of certain social measures foreseen in the Treaty of Rome.

During the negotiations of 1956-7, the French fourth Republic was proud of its character as an advanced Welfare State and fearful of the economic handicaps which it imposed on French industry in competition with socially less advanced partners. Hence the stipulation of art. 119 of the Treaty which committed all Member States to the introduction of equal pay for women during the first transitional stage, and the much vaguer art. 120 which promised to maintain 'the existing equivalence of paid holiday schemes'. Also, a special Protocol on the payment of overtime empowered the French Government to resort to certain safeguards at the end of the first stage, unless overtime payments in the other Community countries were by then at least as generous as they had been in France in 1956.

Equal pay for women (which was again stressed in the Declaration of Intent at the time of the Council's 'acceleration' decision in May, 1960) was by far the most important issue: it was one of the specific conditions for the progress from stage one to stage two, and failure to meet it could thus impede the whole progress of the Community. Following the usual lengthy consultations, the Commission formally recommended to the Member States in July, 1960, that they should ensure the entire exclusion of sex from the standards used for wage fixing (at every level—not only in minimum wage legislation), that no special wage categories for women should be permitted and that no account should be taken in wage calculations of measures specially taken for the protection of working women, even though they might increase production costs.

In the summer of 1961, with only six months to go to the deadline for the earliest possible transition to the second transitional stage, a special working party on the subject was set up under Signor Levi Sandri, President of the Social Affairs Group of the Commission, for an urgent study of the progress made in this field. When the Council settled down in December, 1961, to its heroic attempt to battle through by the end of the year to the second stage, it was clear that little progress had, in fact, been made: France had to accept another bill drawn on the future. The only tangible evidence that its partners were willing to honour their promises was the insertion of yet another date (or dates) in the agreement. Instead of keeping in line with the time table laid down by the Treaty, it was agreed to reach equal pay for women three years later by three instalments. This is another illustration of the Community's practical scale of priorities: in a sphere where the primary beneficiaries of the Treaty are not the dominant business interests (except in a single Member State) but the humblest of workers, 'acceleration' gives way to an almost contemptuous 'go slow'.

Though holidays and overtime were less critically important, the Commission carried out detailed investigations into the factual position in 1956 as the starting point for its unenviable task of interpreting the cryptic text of the Treaty and the subtleties of the Protocol on overtime.

(6) AGRICULTURE

Despite its general bias in favour of a free market economy, the Treaty of Rome is a sufficiently realistic document to approach the difficult and delicate problem of a common agricultural policy from a radically different angle. Instead of pinning its hopes on the abolition of the existing obstacles to agricultural trade, it provided in bold outline a system of managed production and exchange, making use of existing national marketing organizations and supplementing (or even replacing) them in case of need by Community-wide bodies.

The liberalization of agricultural trade was thus linked in principle to the introduction of a common agricultural policy with impeccable objectives. These were to increase agricultural productivity, with special emphasis on an improvement in the use of rural labour, thus ensuring a fair standard of living for the farming population, and to stabilize markets with the effect of ensuring regular supplies and reasonable prices to the consumer.

As these provisions were politically of very great importance, the Treaty was quite specific about procedures and time tables for putting them into effect. The Commission was instructed to convene a conference of Member States 'upon the date of the entry into force of this Treaty' (art. 43(1)); this Conference duly met at Stresa in July, 1958, and laid the foundations for the next step—the preparation of the Commission's proposals for a common agricultural policy. The Treaty allowed two years for this task which was to lead directly to the issue of regulations and other decisions by the Council (art. 43(2)), which had to agree on them unanimously during the first two transitional stages and by a qualified majority thereafter. In cases where the Council decided to set up Community-wide marketing schemes against the wishes of a Member State, they would have to be at least as favourable to the producers as the existing arrangements and would have to treat the whole Community as a single market. During the transitional era, Member States were permitted, under steadily more stringent conditions, to make use of minimum import prices (art. 44) and during the first stage long-term contracts were permissible for certain types of products (art. 45). In circumstances where existing marketing organizations distorted the competitive position, the Commission could fix import or export levies (art. 46).

The Commission's Draft Agricultural Policy

The Commission produced a voluminous first draft of its proposals in November, 1959, while the final draft was published in June, 1960. Though by no means complete within its own frame of reference—the plans for rice and for oils and fats took more than a year longer to complete than the main draft—it is an impressive document which surveys the position of agriculture in the six countries and covers structural policy, market organization and proposals for specific commodities. The commodity chapters are based on detailed summaries of the current situation and show a thorough understanding of the political as well as the economic issues involved, though politics is decorously kept outside the area of discussion and is not permitted to hamstring the Commission's constructive plans.

The outstanding feature of the current position is a widespread dilemma; despite the almost universal use of price supports for certain key commodities which call forth a steadily growing volume of supplies, the system does not succeed in furnishing agricultural producers with living standards comparable to those of the urban population. This relative failure arises from an inefficient structure, with excessive numbers of under-employed smallholders, and from the effect of rising supplies on producer prices.

Structural improvements in agriculture are intimately connected with the Commission's regional development policy for providing underdeveloped and correspondingly poverty-stricken agricultural districts with the necessary 'infra-structure' of roads, power, sanitation and education and with opportunities for non-agricultural employment, where necessary with the help of the European Investment Bank. The areas affected are mainly Southern Italy and parts of Southern and Central France, though other countries also have underdeveloped population pockets. The master plan of the Commission's structural policy is thus the withdrawal of under-employed labour from the land and the creation of efficient 'family' farms by the amalgamation of holdings. The suggested procedure provides for annual factual surveys by the Commission followed by action by the Council on the basis of the Commission's recommendations. National

measures are to be supplemented by a European Fund for structural improvements in agriculture, financed from the Community Budget, which is to form part of a European Agricultural Alignment and Guarantee Fund.

Although in the long-term great emphasis is put on changes
in the structure of agriculture, they must be supplemented by a
common marketing policy aiming at the creation of a single
market for agricultural produce. This involves, in the first place,
a common price level which will be kept by certain devices
above that of the world market where prices 'are still frequently
distorted by artificial measures'.[22] The means adopted for this
purpose differ according to commodities and include direct price
fixing, import duties or variable import levies, or both, as well
as quantitative restrictions. The necessary corollary to this insulation of the common agricultural market from the outside
world is the encouragement of exports by subsidies.

As the creation of an agricultural common market was both
political and economically much more difficult than that of
industrial trade, the procedure for the transitional period was
particularly delicate, as it involved the gradual replacement of
jealously protected national markets by a free internal market,
though in this case freedom was never meant to be complete.
The Treaty provisions for minimum prices, import levies and
long-term contracts indicate the complications foreseen even
during the gestation period of the Community, and the draft
plan proposed that for commodities where a managed market
with 'administered' prices was proposed, the Council should lay
down the principles of price determination (by a qualified
majority), while the Commission should be empowered to fix
annual target prices on the basis of these principles, unless the
Council unanimously chose different prices. This neat attempt
to side-step one of the most explosive issues in the early history
of the Six did not prevent them from almost coming to grief
over this problem when the first practical decisions had to be
taken after a series of delays at the beginning of 1962.

The Commission's long-term plans for individual commodities distinguished three broad groups of products. The
markets for grain, sugar and dairy products were to be secured
by a system of target prices and support prices supplemented by
import levies and, if necessary, import licensing. For meat (beef,

[22] *Third Report*, para. 240.

pig meat, poultry) and for eggs, the main support measure was
to be protection through tariffs, levies or both, with minimum
import prices as a safeguard against exceptionally low-priced
imports. For fruit, vegetables and wine the tariff was to be the
main form of protection, with quality control as a guarantee of
fair competition between the member countries. On the administrative side, separate European Boards were recommended for
grains, sugar, milk and meat and eggs; fruit, vegetables and
wine would be supervised by committees of the heads of the
national grading bodies under the aegis of the Commission.

The preparatory period was to last until June, 1967, with
special time tables for meat and wine, and should be used for a
systematic approach to the common agricultural market step by
step. This would involve equalization of producer prices, co-
ordination of national laws and marketings systems, general
rules of competition, the stimulation of trade within the Community and agreement on a common commercial policy towards
outsiders.

As a first step towards the annual approximation of prices,
the Commission made definite proposals for wheat, barley,
maize and sugar: in July, 1961, the existing price differences
were to be narrowed by adjustments to all or some prices everywhere except in Belgium. In Germany, prices were to go down
for wheat, barley and sugar and to rise for maize; in France,
on the contrary, the price of maize was to come down and the
other prices were to rise, while for Italy an increase in the price
of maize and falls for wheat and sugar were proposed. Smaller
adjustments were envisaged for the Netherlands and Luxembourg. In the case of milk, only the principles of future action
were outlined, and beef prices were to remain free. For a number
of products the use of decreasing levies on trade during
the transition period between the Six was proposed, and this
system was to assume greater prominence during the ensuing
negotiations.

The Agricultural Cockpit

This devolopment was due to the bitter resistance encountered
by the Commission's price adjustment plans in Germany which
generally has the highest price level. Faced with this determined
opposition—which also threatened to block the vital process of
freeing agricultural trade within the Community—the Com-

D

mission changed the emphasis of its earlier schemes by putting the device of gradually declining levies into the centre of its practical proposals. It was hoped that in this way it would be easier to approach the politically difficult aim of direct price adjustments, while cutting through the thicket of trade barriers which proved extremely difficult to remove in isolation. Thus the regulations for grains leave the fixing of target prices (where applicable) to the national authorities and rely for immediate progress on the operation of the variable levy system, while confining themselves to the statement that action will also be needed 'to bring prices into line' and that the levies will decline in step with the approximation in prices.

At the same time, it was hoped to sweep away all existing measures of national protection in relation to intra-Community trade by introducing the declining internal levy as the sole protective device: 'Considering that the trade in agricultural products between Member States is hampered by a series of obstacles, such as customs duties, charges with equivalent effect, quotas and other quantitative restrictions, the progressive abolition of which in the transition period would have, in the absence of harmonizing measures taken by the Community institutions, to be carried out by different procedures and at different speeds; but that, on the other hand, a uniform protective measure at the frontier in intra-Community trade will make possible a progressive reduction of barriers in all the Member States along parallel lines and at a pace which will allow of the gradual establishment of a common agricultural policy . . .'[23]

Apart from extricating the Six, at least temporarily, from the dangerous deadlock over price fixing and the removal of obstacles to the expansion of agricultural trade, the levy system has the great merit of using substantially the same device for internal and international trade: temporarily and on a reducing scale for transactions within the Community, and permanently —and in suitable cases intensified by built-in tariffs—for trade with third countries. The device is also sufficiently flexible, in conjunction with intervention prices and minimum prices called variously 'threshold' and 'sluicegate' prices, to be adapted to the special needs of individual commodities and to make the volume

[23] *Bulletin*, July/August, 1961, p. 123 (Text of the Draft Regulation for the grains sector).

of imports from outside the Community completely dependent on the state of the internal market.

It might therefore have been expected that such a resolutely interventionist and protectionist system, however incompatible with the proclaimed principles and aims of the Common Market, would have been enthusiastically hailed by all the farmers of the Six. In fact, its merits were little appreciated, because technical points were swamped by the bitterly fought clash of opposing interests. The root of the difficulty with the proposed agricultural policy has been from the beginning Germany's reluctance to play the essential part of main importer of the agricultural surpluses of the others (except Belgium) on the scale which they, and particularly the French and the Dutch, regarded as their due under the terms of the Rome Treaty.

Though not nearly so important and complex, Western Germany's interests in agricultural trade vis-à-vis its partners in the Common Market are, by and large, comparable to Britain's interests vis-à-vis the other European countries. The quantitative difference between Germany and Britain in this respect was matched by a radically different approach to the practical solution of the problem. The British Government fatally compromised the chances of success for the Free Trade Area by which it, in effect, countered the challenge of the Common Market by demanding that agriculture should be excluded from its terms, though there might be a possibility of a separate agreement on agricultural trade; even in the absence of other obstacles, such a condition would have condemned the scheme to failure, because it would have been patently unfair to agricultural exporters.

Germany's approach to the Common Market plan was dictated by its great political and economic advantages for the dominant sections of German business, and the German Government preferred to sign first and to bargain afterwards. The stubbornness of Germany's resistance from July, 1960, to January, 1962, to the practical introduction of the common agricultural policy, to which it was legally and morally committed up to the hilt, reflects three factors. The most obvious one is the reluctance of the German farmers to accept a lowering of their domestic prices and a growing volume of agricultural imports from France, Italy and Holland, and the corresponding reluctance of the German Government to antagonize some of its most loyal supporters. Less obvious but at least equally important is the continuing importance of bilateral trade agreements and trade relations between Germany and important suppliers of agricultural products outside the Community which is, in fact, a similar exchange of primary commodities against manufactures as that between Britain and the Commonwealth, though on a smaller scale.

Finally, and perhaps decisively, there is the enormous increase in German power relative to its Common Market partners between 1957 and 1962. Before the signature of the Treaty of Rome, Germany had to make substantial and genuine, if temporary, concessions in order to obtain French approval of the proposed Treaty; in 1962 Germany felt strong enough to haggle about every comma of the commitments undertaken five years ago, and was not even unduly concerned about the threat of a French veto on the progress from the first to the second stage of the Treaty.

The Course of the Negotiations

The clash of interests unleashed by the publication of the Commission's proposals completely upset the rigid time table for the introduction of the common agricultural policy which had been agreed on by the Six only a few weeks earlier as part of the 'acceleration programme'. The Special Committee of the Council which had been proposed originally as part of the procedure for ensuing quick progress in line with the 'Declaration of Intent' of May 12, 1960, became a permanent forum for the continuation of the negotiations on the political level.

After months of hard bargaining, and only just in time to prevent a Dutch veto on the first part of the acceleration programme, the Council took its first decision of substance in December, 1960, when it accepted the principle of the variable levies proposed by the Commission as the main instrument of trade policy for certain (unspecified) commodities. However, it soon became clear that this did not imply a definite commitment to substitute decreasing levies for all existing methods of agricultural protection in intra-Community trade, and throughout 1961 Germany maintained stubbornly its claim to continue with the use of quantitative restrictions and minimum prices towards its Common Market partners.

In addition, and with better reason, Germany contended that

it would be unfair to remove the barriers impeding the flow of trade without at the same time abolishing the distortions of competition only too prevalent in the agricultural field. Thus the German milk producer is protected from foreign competition mainly through import restrictions on butter and certain other dairy products which keep their prices at very much higher levels than in the Netherlands, where the dairy industry is subsidized from public funds to the tune of £30-40m. per year. It can be forcefully argued that the ability of the Dutch milk products manufacturer to undercut his German competitor is less the result of superior efficiency than that of the reduction in the cost of his raw material through massive subsidies; if German import restrictions must go, so must Dutch subsidies. Accepting the basic justification of such arguments, the Commission submitted to the Council in November, 1960, draft regulations on the subject and took a whole series of measures on individual products in the course of 1961 in order to meet German complaints.

On the dominant issue of agreeing a comprehensive common agricultural policy these concessions to the German point of view had very little effect. During the spring and summer, the German representatives played a skilful delaying action by appealing to the political sympathies of their partners with the electoral needs of an outgoing government in an election year, but even when the elections were over the German attitude remained unchanged; in fact, at the meeting of the Council in October, 1961, the German delegation took refuge in the mere quibble that it was not empowered to undertake definite commitments, because no permanent German government was at the moment in office.

Meanwhile it was clear that a final decision could not be delayed much longer. On October 19, 1961, the European Parliament had approved the Commission's draft plan almost unanimously, after a claim to maintain quotas as well as decreasing variable levies in intra-Community trade had been abandoned in order to obtain Socialist approval of the policy as a whole. Some Dutch representatives abstained, because they wished to see specific steps taken in the field of price assimilation which the Commission had deferred owing to their political difficulties. The French Cabinet decided to veto the transition from the first stage to the second stage of the period of transition, not to mention the further acceleration programme, unless a common agricultural policy could be agreed before the end of the year. Moreover, after their unhappy experience with the 'Declaration of Intent' issued by the Council of Ministers on the occasion of the original acceleration decision, the French were unwilling to accept further general assurances on the subject and insisted that on this occasion nothing short of agreed texts would do—a policy dictated no less by the pressure of the French farming community on the government than by Gaullist intransigence and a determination not to be caught twice by the same trick.

The last two months of 1961 thus witnessed an intensely interesting tug of war within the Community which was at first overshadowed in the public mind by the crisis in East-West relations over Berlin but which reached a dramatic climax when the Council of Ministers, completely dropping the pretence of sitting in judgment on the plans prepared by an impartial Commission, engaged in feverish negotiations in order to beat the deadline of December 31, 1961; in the end it was unable to reach agreement before that date and resorted to the legal fiction of stopping the clock on December 29th, and of backdating the agreement reached in the early hours of January 14, 1962, to the beginning of the year.

Apart from the intrinsic importance of the subject, the most momentous feature of this crisis was the fact that, for the first time, the basic strategic principle of the Common Market was called into question—the mutual agreement to satisfy the minimum requirements of all important interests, even though maximum satisfaction was reserved for the dominant business community. That this blow at the very foundation of the edifice came from the strongest economic power which showed for the first time a disconcerting tendency to regard awkward treaties as scraps of paper, after having astonished the world by its moderation in the drafting of the Treaty of Rome and in the opening stages of its operation, may well be felt long after the visible cracks in the Community structure have been successfully papered over.

The Terms of the Compromise

However, for the moment the most important fact was undoubtedly that a compromise was reached. The commodities for which detailed draft regulations had been prepared—cereals, pig meat, eggs and poultry as well as fruit, vegetables and wine— were to be regulated from July, 1962, and a new timetable provided for the submission of similar programmes for rice (April, 1962), milk and beef (May 1, 1962) and sugar (July 15, 1962).

The concessions to the German point of view relate to the length of the period of transition, to the financing of the common fund, to escape clauses and, above all, to prices. The period of transition will last generally until the end of 1969, i.e. twelve years from the date on which the Treaty originally came into force, and the time originally foreseen for reaching the full Community system. Thus the concept of equal treatment for agriculture and industry has been abandoned under German pressure, for the tariff cut on January 1, 1961, embodied the first part of the 'acceleration programme', and an additional ten per cent reduction in duties on mainly non-agricultural products came into force on July 1, 1962.

The financing of the common agricultural fund has been the subject of a short-term bargain for only three years, with the need for unanimous decisions afterwards. The arrangements provide for a supply of funds from the Member States in the same proportion as their liability for contributions to general Community expenses, supplemented on a rising scale by a share of the levies on imports from third countries which accrue in the first place to the importing countries. As part of the fund will be used for structural improvements, Germany's fear that its imports would be burdened with levies for the purpose of subsidising French agricultural exports will be largely disproved, particularly as it has been agreed that Germany's total contributions, whether through budgetary payments or through levies, will not exceed thirty-one per cent, or not much more than its normal share of twenty-eight per cent in Community expenses in general. On the other hand, Germany had to accept the principle that ultimately the fund would be fed entirely from the proceeds of import levies, though not entirely earmarked for agricultural expenditure.

The compromise on escape clauses is particularly ingenious. Except for top-grade fruit and vegetables, an importing country can take action restricting imports on its own initiative, and the Commission must give a ruling on this action within four days. If the Commission disallows the import restriction, it will normally (except for grains) be suspended pending appeal to the Council of Ministers. The formal homage to the supra-national principle as represented by the Commission is thus hedged around by mainly national interests on both sides and, through the device of special Management Committees, even from day to day; the exception for certain grades of perishable fruit and vegetables has been inserted at Italy's request, because in this case a delay of four days would, in fact, be final. The procedure is therefore reversed, with the Commission taking action on complaint from an importing country.

Perhaps the most striking evidence of Germany's bargaining strength is the solution accepted on the pivotal price issue; to speak of a solution is, indeed, a misnomer for the only hard and fast agreement relates to the year 1962-3 for which a price stop has been agreed for both ends of the existing price range. Although in exchange for this acceptance of Germany's minimum demand the principle of price harmonization beginning with the 1963 harvest has been accepted and a further declaration of future aims in this field has been made, the course of events will mainly depend on the balance of power at the time the decisions are made. As Germany can look forward with equanimity towards maintaining its agricultural position as long as the price level of cereals remains approximately where it is now, this settlement may well have more importance than all other items put together.

II

THE COMMUNITY AND
THE GREAT BOOM

FOUR years are a very short time in the life of a new economic
organization; the first four years of the EEC were largely devoted to the running-in of the new institutions and the discussions on the formulation of common policies, and it is too early
to draw any definite conclusions from economic developments
during this period. It is, however, certain that the Community
benefited immensely from the favourable economic climate
during this opening period—materially, politically and psy-
chologically. It is, therefore, of considerable importance to be
clear about the main outline of events in the Community as
a whole and in each of the Member States in order to establish
a factual base from which to consider at least in a provisional
way the complex issue whether, and how far, the Common
Market has been responsible for the economic advance of the
Six and whether the events of the last few years are a reasonably reliable guide for the future.

(1) OUTPUT AND TRADE PATTERNS

The statistics produced by the European Communities are normally based on the year 1958, the first year after the Rome
Treaty came into force and the last year before the initial tariff
reductions between the Six. The choice of this base has the incidental advantages of pitching it rather low, for 1958 was a
year of slow economic growth in some Member States and of a
slight recession in others.

However, there is no good reason for starting from the

assumption that tariff adjustments were the only way in which the Rome Treaty affected the economic life of the Six, and in the following outline 1957 has normally been used as the base year; the Treaty was signed in March of that year and ratified during the summer and there is a large volume of evidence to suggest that many business interests were soon accepting the new state of things and planning on its basis. Where figures for 1961 are available, the use of 1957 as a starting point is particularly convenient, because it lies half-way between 1961 and 1953, the year employed as a base period in most international comparisons on the somewhat questionable assumption that it marked the end of the post-war economic disturbances, the end of the Korean boom and the completion of economic reconstruction in the war-damaged countries of Europe.

During the years under review the index of industrial production as a whole moved generally parallel to that of manufacturing industry, though at a somewhat lower level. The difference between the two is largely due to the poor showing of mining and quarrying in some important countries. Between 1957 and 1961 output in this field dropped sharply in Belgium (by twenty-one per cent) as a result of the depression in the coal industry; it rose only marginally in Germany and increased in the Netherlands by eighteen per cent owing to higher coal production, in Italy by twenty-four per cent and in France by fifty-six per cent owing to the rapid rise of oil and natural gas extraction in these two countries. France was the only one amongst the Six where mining and quarrying expanded more quickly than manufacturing industry.

The best overall view of the extent of the great boom can be obtained from the progress of the index of manufacturing output from year to year:

Table I

Output of manufacturing industries (1953 = 100)

	1957	1958	1959	1960	1961	% increase 1961 over 1957
W. Germany	149	154	166	185	196	32
France	148	156	158	169	177	20
Italy	138	143	159	184	202	46
Netherlands	127	127	140	159	160	26
Belgium	129	122	131	140	145*	12*
Luxembourg	129	125	132	144	148*	15*
EEC	*144*	*148*	*157*	*174*	*186*	*29*
UK	117	116	122	132	133	14

Source: OECD, *General Statistics*   *estimated

Between 1953 and 1957, before the establishment of the EEC, the rise in manufacturing industry was steepest in Germany and France and smallest in Benelux, with hardly any difference between the Netherlands and Belgium-Luxembourg; Italy stood half-way between the two groups. Between 1957 and 1961 Italy advanced most quickly, followed by Germany and during 1959 and 1960 by the Netherlands. The rate of progress in France was much slower, while Belgium and Luxembourg recovered late from the setback suffered in the depression of 1958.

The main expansionary force came from the chemical, metals and engineering industries, while the traditional consumer goods industries, food and particularly textiles, expanded much less quickly and in some cases not at all.

Table II

Increase in manufacturing industries 1957-1960
(in per cent of 1957)

	All Manufactures	Food etc.	Textiles	Basic Metals	Metal Goods	Chemicals
W. Germany	24	10	4	21	33	44
France	14	11	—2	16	13	54
Italy	33	14	15	25	35	55
Netherlands	25	13	5	39	46	15
Belgium	7	8	—4	14	3	13
Luxembourg	12	25		16		—6
EEC	21	9	4	20	26	46
UK	14	9	—6	10	14	26

Calculated from OECD, *General Statistics*

France and Belgium, the laggards during the three-year period covered by the table, were well below the average in every category with the exception of the French food and chemical industries; Italy beat the average in every group. Despite the substantial share of 'consumer durables' (motor cars, refrigerators, television sets, etc.) in the metal goods category, the figures show the familiar features of an investment boom. This reflected partly the strength of the internal demand for investment goods and partly the extremely buoyant export trade in these products.

For even a glance at the following table indicates the large share of foreign trade in this massive industrial advance, with exports expanding much more quickly than manufacturing output. The figures again show large differences between the performance of individual countries but with another pattern than in the case of manufacturing output, though in view of the varying importance of non-industrial exports the comparison

Table III
Volume of total Exports
(1953 = 100)

	1957	1958	1959	1960	1961	% increase 1961 over 1957
W. Germany	188	195	222	255	269	43
France	131	137	164	192	202*	54*
Italy	178	189	232	280	336	89
Netherlands	136	147	165	187	196	44
Belgium-L.	133	136	154	168	180*	35*
EEC	156	163	189	219	233	49
UK	121	116	121	128	131	8

Source: OECD—*General Statistics*
*estimated

can only be used in a very rough and ready way.

During the four years preceding the Common Market, exports rose more quickly than manufacturing output in all Member States except France. Germany was again in the first place, while Benelux was again near the bottom, but Italy almost equalled Germany's expansion, an indication of the extent to which Italy's economic growth depends on foreign trade. During the last four years, the rise in exports exceeded the rise in manufacturers throughout the Six: Italy's exports expanded much faster than those of any other member country, followed by France and, much lower down the scale, by Germany and the Netherlands, with Belgium in last place.

However, global comparisons of this kind are far too primitive to be of much use; for a more detailed analysis, the commodity pattern and geographical distribution of foreign trade must be taken into account. In the absence of full details for 1961, the salient features can be obtained by a comparison between 1957 and 1960, though a more detailed summary of the figures for individual years will be given later (Table VIII).

Table IV
Increase in the value of foreign trade—EEC 1957-60
(in per cent of 1957)

	Food, Drink, Tobacco	Raw Materials*	Fuel	Equipment	Other Manufact.	Total
IMPORTS						
within EEC	33	32	6	52	57	44
third countries	5	—2	—17	41	52	10
Total	11	2	—13	46	54	20
EXPORTS						
within EEC	34	32	6	48	55	43
third countries	4	9	—	50	25	28
Total	16	22	3	49	34	33

*incl. oils and fats   calculated from OEEC—*Foreign Trade Statistics*

There is no mistaking the vigorous general expansion, with exports far outstripping imports. Even more striking is the different experience for primary commodities and manufactured products, though in the case of agricultural produce individual years can always be affected by weather conditions. In 1957, total imports of food, raw materials and fuel accounted for over $15,700m. out of total imports valued at $24,763m.; three years later, their value had risen by only about $150m., while total imports had gone up by almost $5,000m. to $29,621 m. Virtually the total rise in imports was due to equipment and other manufactures.

On the export side, the Community had always been more important as a supplier of industrial products than of primary commodities which accounted for only a quarter of the total value of exports and contributed less than $750m. or just over ten per cent to the total increase of over $7,300m. in three years.

As the terms of trade during this period favoured the advanced industrial countries everywhere, this predominance of manufactures in the expansion of foreign trade, however complete, is not unexpected. On the other hand, the shift towards intra-Community trade must be described as striking by any standard. In broad terms, total imports from third countries during this period of unparalleled prosperity rose by ten per cent in three years, while trade between member countries expanded by forty-four per cent. (In 1961, the increase in imports from third countries over the previous year amounted to five per cent compared with fifteen per cent for intra-Community trade.) Exports to third countries rose between 1957 and 1960 by twenty-eight per cent or almost three times as fast as imports from these sources; in 1961 the increase in exports to the outside world fell below five per cent, compared with fourteen per cent in 1960, which may be important as a pointer to a change in economic climate.

The faster expansion of intra-Community trade compared with imports from other sources held good for each main category. Imports of food, beverages and tobacco from third countries rose between 1957 and 1960 by five per cent in value compared with thirty-three per cent within the EEC. Similarly, intra-Community trade in raw materials, oils and fats rose by one-third, while the value of outside imports actually declined fractionally. The contraction in imports from third countries was most spectacular for fuel, helped by the shipping slump, the fall in coal and oil prices from their post-Suez pinnacles and by German restrictions on coal imports, while the value of fuel traded between member countries registered a modest rise. Although manufactured imports from all sources expanded rapidly, the rate of increase was somewhat higher for intra-Community trade than for other imports.

As with imports so—generally—with exports. Food exports to third countries stagnated even more completely than imports from them, and the rise in the value of raw material exports to them, though not negligible, was only a fraction of the growth of trade between the members. Fuel exports to the outside world were maintained much more successfully than outsiders' exports to the Six, but nevertheless fell marginally. Only the export of equipment (machinery and transport equipment) to the outside world rose at about the same rate as internal exchanges, but for other manufactures the difference in favour of the EEC was again pronounced.

These figures for the Community as a whole thus supply the outlines of a fascinating picture; it can be filled in to some extent by a comparison of the contrasting experience of the individual member countries.

Table V

EEC countries: Increase in Dollar Value of Imports and Exports
(in per cent)

	(i) 1960 over 1957			(ii) 1961 over 1960)		
IMPORTS	*intra* *EEC*	*other*	*total*	*intra* *EEC*	*other*	*total*
W. Germany	71	24	35	13	6	8
France	41	—8	3	14	3	6
Italy	68	20	31	17	8	11
Netherlands	23	2	10	21	6	13
Belgium-L.	28	7	16	12	11	6
EEC	*44*	*10*	*20*	*15*	*5*	*9*
EXPORTS						
W. Germany	34	33	33	19	8	11
France	60	28	36	19	$-\frac{1}{2}$	5
Italy	71	36	45	21	12	15
Netherlands	41	22	30	11	3	7
Belgium-L.	31	10	19	9	—2	4
EEC	*43*	*28*	*33*	*16*	*5*	*9*

calculated from OOEC, *Foreign Trade Statistics* and
EEC *Allgemeines Statistisches Bulletin*

On the import side, Germany and France occupy extreme positions: between 1957 and 1960 Germany had the steepest rise, French imports as a whole barely changed in dollar terms, with a large rise in imports from its EEC partners almost balanced by a drop in imports from the rest of the world including the Franc area. Of the other countries, Italy's imports rose in a similar manner to Germany's, at a slightly lower rate between 1957 and 1960, rather more quickly in 1961. In the first three years Benelux, and particularly Dutch, imports rose much less than those of Germany and Italy, and in the case of intra-Community trade also much less than those of France; in 1961 Dutch imports rose more than in the whole of 1957-1960.

The export position was rather more complex. German exports between 1957 and 1960 rose at the same rate both to EEC countries and to the outside world. (In 1961, a much stronger expansion in exports to the Community became apparent.) Italy and France raised their exports to the other member countries by almost three-quarters and three-fifths in three years, in both cases about twice the rate of increase in exports to third countries. In 1961 their exports to the EEC rose at a similar rate, but while Italy did well in exports to third countries, France showed a marginal drop. Dutch exports in 1957-60 developed similarly to Germany's but with a greater reliance on the Six; in 1961 Dutch exports to all destinations slowed down considerably. Belgium increased exports to the Community between 1957 and 1960 at three times the rate to other markets, while in 1961 Belgian exports to third countries fell by two per cent. Germany's experience, at least during the first three years under review, differed markedly from that of its partners in relying much less on the* Community for its exports, while acting to a much greater extent as a market for the other member countries.

Even such a tentative and superficial analysis indicates the need for a separate discussion of the individual countries composing the Community. Although the Common Market in its initial stage was mainly concerned with trade exchanges, these were intimately connected with the economic conditions in each of the Member States. Thus it is impossible to assess the provisional effects of the Community in the economic field without a closer look at its components.

(2) THE ILL-MATCHED PARTNERS

Western Germany

The causes of the German economic miracle have been traced more or less exhaustively in a massive literature. When the Treaty of Rome was signed in March, 1957, Germany, though deprived of its Eastern provinces, was again the strongest economic power on the Continent of Europe west of Russia, with a formidable heavy industrial base in the Ruhr, well-developed processing industries, an excellent transport system and a highly protected but far from unproductive agriculture. Foreign demand for German manufactures was buoyant and the gold and dollar reserves were high and rising at an embarrassing rate.

Between 1950 and 1955 Germany's gross national product had increased more quickly than that of any other Western country, but this could well be attributed to a quick recovery from the abysmal depth to which the German economy had fallen in the immediate post-war era. By 1955 this stage had, however, been left behind, and henceforward valid comparisons could be made between Germany's progress and that of countries with a less unfortunate post-war experience. Yet between 1955 and 1960 Germany's rate of material growth again outstripped that of all other European countries outside the Soviet block (as well as Canada and the United States): with 6.1 per cent per year it was approached within the Six only by Italy (5.9 per cent), completely overshadowing the very respectable record of France and the Netherlands (4.2 per cent), not to mention Belgium's low average increase of 2.4 per cent per year.[1]

This rate of growth coincided with, and was largely due to, the high share of investment in the use of national resources. Gross investment was almost twenty-three per cent of national output in 1950, when the reconstruction process was in full swing, but far from gradually falling it rose further with the years, exceeding twenty-four per cent in 1957 and twenty-six per cent in 1960.[2] The bulk of this investment took the form of fixed assets which were largely net additions to the stock of productive capital, because German industry started practically

[1] EEC, *Allgemeines Statistisches Bulletin*, October, 1961, p. 10.
[2] EEC, *Allg. Stat. Bull.*, Dec., 1961, p. 36.

from scratch in 1948 and the share of replacements in capital formation was therefore exceptionally low.

This prominence of capital investment corresponds to the large share of profits in the national income which is reflected rather than measured by the fabulous rise in share values. This type of investment remained untouched by the currency reform of 1948, which wiped out well over ninety per cent of all monetary savings, and stock exchange values soon started going up. They rose by more than half between 1950 and 1953, doubling again during the next two years; 1956 and 1957 were years of doubt, with the index moving narrowly at about twice the 1953 level, but from the middle of 1958 shares began to soar and rose without any real interruption until their all-time peak in August, 1960, when the index reached 864 (1953=100) or almost fourteen times its 1950 level. They then faltered and declined, not without sustained recovery attempts, until at the end of 1961 they stood about twenty-five per cent below the peak, with a further decline in the first half of 1962.

This change in the temper of the stock market corresponded to the growing obstacles to further economic expansion through the progressive exhaustion of resources and, above all, the tightening labour supply. The growing tension between Germany and the East endangered the main source of fully effective additional labour even before the erection of the East Berlin Wall in August, 1961, while internal labour resources were practically exhausted. Although East Germans were the largest 'foreign' group, there were sizeable contingents of workers from other neighbouring countries amongst the 520,000 workers from abroad, including over 40,000 Dutchmen and 25,000 Austrians, but Germany's expanding industrial machine sucked in workers by the hundred thousands from more distant quarters in peace no less than in war. German recruiting officers scoured not only Italy and Spain but Greece and Turkey for hands willing to turn the wheels of the economic miracle, and German wage rates at last showed definite signs of outstripping the rise in productivity—not owing to any show of militancy by the Trade Unions but simply in response to the play of the forces of supply and demand.

High (but relatively stable) prices, high profits and relatively low wages had been the popular recipe of the popular Minister of Economics, Dr Erhard, for the reconstruction of the dis-

E

organized and largely destroyed German economic machine. The German working class was doubly cowed by the traumatic experience of the Hitler era and by the uninviting alternative of the mock-socialism of the East German regime. In addition it was disciplined even in a period of economic expansion by the 'industrial reserve army' pouring in across the zone boundaries. Thus it was working with a will and reasonably satisfied with the steady rise in nominal and real wages, even though its share in the national income rose little up to 1960. Between 1953 and 1957 gross wages increased by about thirty per cent, but with productivity climbing by twenty-six per cent the labour cost per unit of output changed very little and during the next two years it even tended to decline. However, between the end of 1959 and the end of 1961 hourly earnings jumped by twenty-one per cent and despite the continuing improvement in productivity as a result of heavy capital investment wage costs per unit of production were rising fast almost for the first time since the start of the economic miracle.

Despite the rapid growth in German imports between 1957 and 1960 (to an increasing extent from other members of the Six), German exports to third countries rose much more quickly than imports; thus the active trade balance with the Community declined by half (from $740m. to $351m.), while the credit balance on Germany's trade with the outside world went up from $336m. to $961m. The large hoard of foreign exchange in German banks had threatened the precarious international monetary balance even before the Common Market, but its main cause—the huge surplus on foreign trade without corresponding capital exports—continued to operate. In addition, the German balance of payments benefited from the large dollar (and the smaller but still substantial sterling) disbursements for the maintenance of American and British troops on German soil and was reinforced, from time to time, by a massive surplus on capital account. This was partly due to the attraction of the economic miracle for foreign investments but largely to recurring bouts of short-term speculation, for the hope of capital gains from a revaluation of the Deutsche Mark acted as a magnet on 'hot money' from many sources.

After heated internal discussions (but without consultation with Germany's Common Market partners), the German government revalued the currency in March, 1961, by the relatively small amount of 4¾ per cent, from 4.20 DM to 4 DM to the US dollar (11.76 to 11.20 DM to the £). The short term effect of this measure was, paradoxically enough, an increase in the surplus of the balance of payments, for imports rose less than anticipated, while exports increased at first only slightly in price without becoming, for the time being, uncompetitive. During the first two months of 1962, however, the export surplus almost disappeared. In the long run, even the modest revaluation of March, 1961, is bound to strengthen the forces making for a moderation, and ultimately an end, of the German boom which has been the most powerful engine of Europe's economic expansion during the last decade.

This boom has been of enormous benefit to the other member countries of the EEC during its first stage from 1958 to 1961. The apparently insatiable world demand for German manufactures provided them with unexpectedly easy opportunities of stepping up their exports to Germany without feeling the full force of German competition in their own home markets. Germany increased imports of food and raw materials from the Six mainly at the expense of other suppliers—and even so the other Member States were bitterly dissatisfied with their relatively slow rates of progress. (The value of German imports of food, drink and tobacco from the EEC rose by thirty-five per cent between 1957 and 1960 compared with six per cent from other sources; raw material imports increased by forty-five per cent from the EEC and 0.3 per cent from third countries.) The growth of German industrial imports exceeded the most optimistic expectations, for in the space of three short years the other Common Market countries trebled their sales of equipment and doubled those of other manufactures to Germany, in both cases a multiple of the advances made by Germany's other suppliers.

France

The issue which exercised the minds of economists and politicians amongst the Six more than any other between the signature of the Treaty of Rome and the date fixed for the first round of duty reductions was the willingness and ability of the French government to fulfil its obligations under the Treaty.

M. Mollet's government, whose foreign minister signed for France, had been enthusiastically 'European', but by then it had taken its inglorious place in the limbo of fallen French ministries and the Fourth Republic itself had ceased to exist. General de Gaulle and his supporters had never been amongst the advocates of a Federal Europe which inspired at least some of the founding fathers of the Community. However, once in power the new regime quickly satisfied the Six on the score of its willingness to accept the Treaty while strenuously resisting all attempts at widening it into a European Free Trade Area.

What remained in doubt until the last day was the ability of the French economy to do without the numerous restrictions on foreign trade and to accept even a ten per cent cut in duties on imports from the other Member States; these doubts might well have been reinforced by the far-reaching moves towards full currency convertibility by a number of countries announced shortly before the fateful New Year of 1959. In fact, French determination to fall in line with the economic philosophy behind the Treaty of Rome as well as with its specific obligations was made emphatically clear on December 28, 1958, by the measures of the Minister of Finance, M. Pinay, taken on the basis of the Rueff Report.

The new economic policy combined fairly sweeping measures of trade liberalization with a further devaluation of the currency—the second in less than eighteen months, for the emergency steps of July, 1957, were, in fact, a partial devaluation—and with a resolutely deflationary domestic policy. In terms of economic growth, the price exacted by this policy was severe: if the international recession of 1958 had slowed down the rise in the volume of the gross national product to a mere 1.8 per cent, Government policy was responsible for keeping it as low as 2.5 per cent in 1959, when the European boom was already gathering speed; it was only in 1960, when the boom was at its height, that the French national product rose by 6.1 per cent, though this included substantial (and partly involuntary) stockpiling. At a time when Germany, Italy and the Netherlands vigorously forged ahead, France thus marked time for almost two years. The stagnation of 1958-59 was also the main cause of the incomplete success of the 'Third Plan' which budgeted for a rise of twenty-seven per cent in the gross domestic product (twenty per cent for agriculture and thirty to thirty-seven per cent for industry); the outturn has been estimated at twenty-two per cent (eighteen per cent for agriculture and twenty-eight per cent for industry).[3]

The essence of the Pinay-Rueff policy was an improvement in the international competitive position of French exports and a damping down of imports and of internal purchasing power. In this it was almost completely successful. The devaluations of 1957-58 increased the cost of imports but reduced their volume by one per cent in 1958 and by a further two per cent in 1959, before a sharp rise in 1960. Though their value in domestic currency rose by thirty per cent between 1957 and 1960, their dollar value declined in 1958 and 1959 and exceeded the 1957 figure only in 1960. Exports of goods and services, on the other hand, forged steadily ahead and rose in volume by four per cent in 1958, ten per cent in 1959 and fourteen per cent in 1960,[4] thus transforming a chronically passive balance of trade into a substantial surplus which put an end to the frequent foreign exchange crises which had done so much to demoralize the French economy during the preceding decade.

This great success was obtained through the virtual cessation of growth in consumer expenditure during 1958 and 1959 which expanded (in real terms) by 0.6 per cent in 1958 and 1.7 per cent in 1959 and only in 1960, a year of great prosperity, a more substantial increase of 5.4 per cent was achieved.[5] Its value in current prices rose, indeed, from year to year by ten per cent or more, but this was mainly the result of rising prices caused by devaluation which was most directly felt in the prices of manufactures and thereby contributed prominently to the tension between town and countryside: between 1958 and 1961 the industrial wholesale price index rose by fourteen per cent (i.e. roughly the amount of the devaluation in December, 1958), while agricultural wholesale prices increased by only four per cent.

The multiplicity of French price indices, with different components and using different base periods, makes direct comparisons suitably difficult, but the following table provides some measure of the relative economic fortunes of different social groups:

[3] L'Année Politique (Paris, 1961), p. 168.
[4] EEC, Allg. Stat. Bull., Dec., 1961, p. 44.
[5] ibid.

Table VI

French Prices and Wages (1957 = 100)

	1958	1959	1960	end March 1961
PRICES:				
General Wholesale	111.5	116.8	120.2	121.5
Farmers'	121.3	114.3	119.1	117.8
Retail (250 articles)	115.1	122.1	126.6	128.9
WAGES AND SALARIES:				
Minimum wages	113.5	120.9	124.8	126.9
Private economy (hourly)	111.9	119.0	126.9	133.7
Government (monthly)	116.4	126.5	131.1	137.0
"REAL" WAGES AND SAL:				
Private economy	97.2	97.5	100.2	103.7
Government	101.1	103.5	103.5	106.3

calculated from OEEC, *France*, July 1961. p. 38

To measure farmers' prices against any other price index is always arbitrary, though this was how they were calculated under the system of 'indexation' to compensate them for higher input costs and which was swept away by M. Pinay in December, 1958. There is reason to believe that they had done extremely well under this system, and the following years saw a sharp cut in farmers' prices which were in mid 1961 back to their 1958/9 level and out of line with the increase in general wholesale prices, the cost of living and wage rates since 1957.

The effect of the government's economic policy on wages is also plain: though money wages rose in 1958 and 1959, they lagged behind the cost of living; despite prosperity and full employment, average real wages in the private economy as a whole (and particularly the earnings of wage earners with large families) were below the 1957 level until well into 1960—as good an illustration of a 'wage pause' as any seen in recent years. Only the remuneration of government employees kept steadily ahead of retail prices, with net money salaries in 1961 no less than thirty-seven per cent up on 1957 and real salaries six per cent higher. These variations in the economic fortunes of some social groups may well reflect the change in the political balance of power between the Fourth Republic and its successor.

The national income figures are not sufficiently detailed to permit a statistical analysis of the experience of the business community, and the movement of share indices is only a crude illustration of the changes in its position. For what it is worth, it shows a rise of over a quarter in 1959 over 1958 followed by a further eighteen per cent in 1960 and seventeen per cent in 1961, despite the autumn setback triggered off by the growing political tension over Berlin. Further advances took place early in 1962, particularly after the Evian agreement with the Algerian nationalists.

The political basis of De-Gaulle-Pinay's 'new economic policy' was the grave defeat suffered by the French workers, whatever their political and trade union affiliation, by the fall of the Fourth Republic and the creation of a strong bureaucratic government. The independence of the new regime of parliamentary criticism and its immunity from parliamentary displeasure is demonstrated most clearly by its determination to deal as firmly with the peasant-farmers as with the workers, while creating the right atmosphere for the business classes to make use of the opportunities of the Common Market in these unexpectedly favourable conditions.

Yet only on the most short-sighted view is it possible to cast a neat balance of economic gain and social loss while ignoring the frightening political debit balance of the Fifth Republic. The French working classes were fairly effectively eliminated from the political struggle with the collapse of the Fourth Republic, and the disreputable manoeuvres of Communists and Socialists, which had become little more than rival party machines, have lost what little importance they once may have had. Economic dissatisfaction amongst the industrial workers during the prolonged 'pause' took the form of industrial guerilla action rather than that of large-scale strikes, and the elimination of the Left from political influence has not created a new balance but left a dangerous vacuum.

The French farmers on the other hand—many of them Gaullists before the event—took less meekly to the new forms of financial discipline, and their riots and disobedience campaigns have been much more in evidence than the sporadic strikes of certain key sections of the workers. The result of this undertone of opposition, whether mute or articulate, has been the growing power of the bureaucracy, represented in its most palpable and distasteful form by the arbitrary and lawless force of the police in its dealings with most types of political disaffection.

Against the background of the Algerian crisis, of an extreme

Right in active rebellion and of an army permanently on the verge of succumbing to the wooing of its extremist leaders, the prevalence of apathy and cynicism amongst the majority of the French people may exact a heavy price from France's future for M. Pinay's and M. Rueff's economic miracle, mark II.

Italy

The economic development of post-war Italy is even more impressive than that of Western Germany. In particular, during the second part of the 1950s Italy has enjoyed a remarkable economic revival and its rate of expansion (5.9 per cent per year) was only imperceptibly lower than during 1950-55 (6.0 per cent). In fact, the yearly growth of the gross national product per head of the population was identical in both periods (5.3 per cent), and during 1955-60 it was the highest in Europe.[6] Furthermore, the growth continued at a fairly steady pace year after year, with only a moderate slowing-down during the recession of 1958 and a comparatively gentle quickening of the pace in the boom year of 1960. In both years, the crucial change occurred in fixed investment which expanded on average by nine per cent annually, or half as much again as the national product as a whole. In 1958 fixed investment increased by only 1.4 per cent and the growth of the national product was limited to 4.4 per cent, largely due to an unusually good agricultural season; the boom of 1960 raised investment by no less than 14.9 per cent over 1959, and total output increased by 6.1 per cent.[7]

The Italian economic system has two peculiar features, one long-standing, the other of more recent origin. The co-existence of a fairly well-developed industrial system in the North and Centre and an abysmally poor and backward agriculture in the South and the large islands of Sardinia and Sicily has been in evidence at least since the *risorgimento*. The combination of a robust 'market economy' with only moderate claims to social welfare and of large-scale national ownership of industry, though not without historical precedent, is of more recent origin. Apart from the traditional government monopolies administered as part of the normal bureaucratic system (railways, posts, telephone and telegraph, salt and tobacco), State-owned corporations controlled in 1957 a quarter of the output of electricity,

[6] EEC, *Allg. Stat. Bull.*, Oct. 1961, p.10.   [7] *ibid.*, Dec., 1961, p. 44.

fifteen per cent of the merchant navy, fifty-five per cent of steel production, over one-tenth of mechanical engineering, almost all the natural gas, ten to fifteen per cent of oil and twenty per cent of refining capacity, employing altogether 287,000 workers.[8]

The key role in Italy's industrial expansion was played by industries largely in public hands—steel, oil and natural gas. Particularly the dramatic switch from coal to oil and gas in Europe's energy supply during the later 1950s has held out the hope of permanent advance for a country such as Italy which is practically without coal resources but well endowed with gas and, at least potentially, with oil and with a thrusting publicly-owned corporation under able and determined leadership.

Politically, the strength and pivotal importance of nationalized industry is something of a paradox, for like Western Germany Italy has been governed throughout the post-war era by the Christian Democrats in temporary alliances with some of the smaller parties, though Alcide de Gasperi, the Italian Dr Adenauer, has failed to provide the personal continuity of political direction supplied by his German counterpart. By and large, the economic policy of successive Italian governments has been no less favourable to the business interests than that of the Adenauer-Erhard governments, and their determination to maintain this relationship has been tested rather more severely.

Like Germany, Italy had to carry the social burden, and reaped the industrial benefits, of a large reservoir of unemployed man power. The backward South provided willing, if ill-trained, hands for the industrial expansion in the North, as well as a surplus of migratory workers who swarmed well beyond the French and Swiss borders in search of a livelihood: unskilled factory jobs in Germany, coal mining in Belgium and even construction works in Luxembourg were manned increasingly by Italian workers who must have accounted for the major part of the million of migrant workers for which the Social Affairs Department of the European Commission is assuming growing responsibilities.

Within the framework of industrial expansion, the low wages of Italian labour are a competitive asset for Italian industry; and not only was the absolute level of industrial wages in Italy

[8] EEC, *Report on the Economic Situation in the Countries of the Community* (Brussels, 1958), p. 373.

below that of other member countries (except the Netherlands), but their rate of growth was also slower. Between 1953 and 1958, gross hourly wages in manufacturing industry rose in Germany by thirty-eight per cent, in France by fifty-eight per cent, in the Netherlands by fifty-one per cent, in Belgium by thirty-one per cent and in the United Kingdom by thirty-seven per cent; the rate for Italy was twenty-eight per cent, and only in the case of France was the effect of this difference on the competitive position of Italian exports balanced by a change in the parity of the currency. Since then Italy has continued to lag behind Germany, France and Holland, though wage rates went up more quickly than in Belgium.[9]

The impetus of the revolution in the power base of the economy and the ample supply of cheap and intelligent labour was accompanied by a renaissance of Italian leadership in taste for many consumer goods ranging from the styling of clothes and shoes to that of car bodies. Particularly in the leather and textile industries, which were almost invariably amongst the laggards in the other member countries and in the United Kingdom, Italy managed to show steady progress both before and after the establishment of the Common Market.

Although important elements of Italy's economic good fortune during the 1950s give promise of permanent advance, the position of the country is far from secure. Internally, there is not only the patchy building record (the number of dwelling-rooms finished was 102,000 in 1957 and 106,000 in 1960), the insufficient investment in public transport and the heritage of poverty in general but particularly the enormous problem of the South. This remains one of the great backward areas of Europe, though the discovery of large gas deposits (and the hope of oil) may in the long run give powerful support to the efforts of the *Cassa per il Mezzogiorno*.

In the export trade, progress in important industries may well have been that of the marginal producer who benefits disproportionately in times of boom but whose position in times of recession is correspondingly precarious. This may become a grave handicap as a result of Italy's heavy dependence on the great German boom in three crucial respects. Germany takes more than one-sixth of Italy's total exports—a higher proportion than for any Member State of the Six except the Nether-

[9] OECD, *General Statistics*, March, 1962, p. 37, EEC, *Allg. Stat. Bull.*

lands—and a sharp recession in the German market could hit Italian exports severely, for they are far from irreplaceable. Even more important is Germany's part in providing two of the most important sources of Italy's 'invisible' income needed in order to cover the passive balance of commodity trade— tourism and the earnings of Italian emigrants. In 1960, trade in goods resulted in an adverse balance of $893m., while gross receipts from tourism were $625m. and emigrants' remittances $288m., a total of $913m.[10] Germans are by far the largest contingent amongst Italy's foreign visitors, and German industry has become a magnet for large numbers of Italians in search of lucrative jobs abroad. In addition, Germany may well account for a sizeable part of foreign capital invested in Italy which exceeded $300m. in 1960.

Despite all these reservations there can be no doubt about the enormous economic advance of Italian industry during the last ten years and particularly during the recent boom—nor about the radically uneven distribution of its benefits amongst the different classes of society. Although industrial workers as a class are in a much better position than the peasants to obtain part of the fruits of economic progress, their share has been meagre by any standard but particularly by comparison with the fabulous gains made by the owners of Italian industry. Between 1953 and 1958, industrial wages went up by twenty-eight per cent, half of which was accounted for by rising prices, while average stock market values increased by seventy per cent—a large but not, perhaps, an unusual discrepancy; during the next two years, however, shares went up on average by no less than 130 per cent, after a peak rise of 200 per cent in September, 1960, and even after the inevitable setback they remained about 130 per cent higher than in 1958, while hourly gross wages increased by sixteen per cent between 1958 and the summer of 1961 accompanied by a four per cent rise in the cost of living (including a jump in rents by thirty-eight per cent).

Despite their modest material benefits in a period of unparalleled prosperity, the industrial workers of the North and Centre belong to the fortunate, if not the privileged, sections of Italian society. The underprivileged substratum of the Italian people is the peasantry of the South—and progress in the task of transforming this gigantic rural slum into an active part of

[10] OEEC, *Italy* (1961), p. 26.

modern society has been painfully slow, though some progress
is undoubtedly being made. Though easily forgotten, this permanent *momento* of Italy's structural weakness is a necessary
corrective to the complacent view of its astonishing industrial
advance and an indication of the precarious basis of its prosperity.

Netherlands

Devastated on a serious scale during the second world war
after generations of peace, the Netherlands reached the lowest
point in their political fortunes with the loss of their Indonesian
Empire. After more than three centuries they almost found
themselves back at their starting point: a small (but quickly
increasing) people in a small corner of Western Europe.

To the onlooker the loss of Indonesia, important though it
had been to the Dutch as a source of wealth, may well appear
a blessing in disguise, for it provided the initial shock for their
economic rehabilitation during the post-war era. Their remain-
ing wealth, their ancient skills as farmers and sailors, bankers
and traders played their part in this process, but its core was
the extensive industrialization of the country based on the
systematic control of wages at a level well below that of other
comparable nations, and above all below that of Holland's
Benelux partner Belgium.

Industrialization went hand in hand with a re-orientation of
trade and industry. Traditionally a high proportion of Dutch
industry was concerned with the processing of materials from
and for tropical countries, but without in any way abandoning
these trades, the Dutch intensified their economic links with
their neighbours to the South and East—Belgium-Luxembourg
and Western Germany.

Although less formal than the link with Belgium, the connection with Germany grew steadily closer. Dutch agriculture had
always looked to the Ruhr basin as its natural market, Dutch
shipping found its obvious function in transporting goods to
and from Germany along the Rhine route, and with the revival
of the German economy Holland's big Eastern neighbour played
a growing part as a source of imports and a market for Dutch
exports. The German orientation of the Dutch economy became
steadily more pronounced since 1958, when Germany replaced
Belgium as the Netherlands' best customer. In 1960 more than

twenty-two per cent of all Dutch exports went to Germany, and exports form a higher proportion of national output in the Netherlands than in any other European country. The value of Dutch exports to Germany amounted in 1960 to almost eight per cent of the Dutch gross national product, and the Netherlands became to a considerable extent the direct subcontractor for German industries bulging with export orders to all parts of the globe, particularly in the engineering industries.

During the last decade the Netherlands benefited enormously from this favourable Eastern trade wind, and although the annual growth in the national product slackened from 5.6 per cent in 1950-55 to 4.2 per cent in 1955-60, even the lower figure represents an unusually high rate of progress. It was supported by a rising population and a very high rate of investment (in which foreign investment played a far from negligible part) and vitally depended on a prodigious expansion in foreign trade.

The monetary reflection of the Great Boom brought the most striking demonstration of the extent to which the Dutch economy had become integrated into the German economic system with the revaluation of the guilder in March, 1961, immediately after that of the Deutsche Mark and by the same percentage (4¾ per cent). Although the economy showed similar symptoms to the German, it is far from clear that they warranted such a step, but the Dutch authorities had no genuine freedom of choice. The balanced and rather dehydrated comment of the OEEC experts was that it could be explained 'as much by anxiety to maintain internal stability as by a desire to reduce external surpluses . . . Its chief advantage will be to ensure a better parity between Netherlands' prices and foreign prices'.[11] The reason for this measure was, not of course, any fear that Dutch prices were uncompetitive with 'foreign' (ie. principally German) prices, but that a relative fall of five per cent in Dutch prices would have sucked an ever-growing share of Dutch labour and goods into the vortex of the German boom, while the simultaneous rise in the price of imports from Germany would have given another twist to the inflationary spiral in the country.

However inevitable in the circumstances, the re-alignment of the guilder not only demonstrates its position as an economic satellite of the Deutsche Mark but must also be regarded as yet another hostage to fortune, more precisely to the indefinite con-

[11] OEEC, *Benelux* (1961), p. 68.

tinuation of the German boom, because it will make it more difficult to adjust the Dutch economy to its end, not to mention the consequences of a recession in the German economy.

The specially close relationship between the Netherlands and Western Germany gives rather more significance to the change of trend in Dutch industry and foreign trade since the spring of 1961 than would belong to it in more normal conditions. The Netherlands have continued to ride on a wave of high prosperity, but what happened was not simply a welcome slackening of the boom but a drop in output to or below that of the previous year. Until April, 1961, industrial production was running well ahead of the previous year, with only a slight falling-off in the rate of advance, while exports were forging ahead even faster. From May, 1961, onwards, production trends changed course, so sharply that the actual level of output declined, with a few exceptions, to that of 1960. Most of these exceptions were in consumption goods industries and in the chemical industry and the gap between current performance and the results of early 1961 has been most noticeable in the trend leader, the metal working industries, where output has been falling slightly in 1961 when a year ago it was rising. Though partly due to the reduction in working hours in the summer of 1961, this change also reflected the effect of revaluation on Holland's competitive position.

The Central Planning Bureau forecast for 1961 a rise of 'only' 5½ per cent for manufacturing output, following an increase of thirteen per cent in 1960; the corresponding figures for the metal working industries were nine and nineteen per cent. In fact, the index figures show a rise of less than one per cent for the year, following increases of five per cent or more in its opening months. Although exports have not fallen off since May in comparison with 1960, their volume increased in 1961 by less than five per cent (compared with over thirteen per cent in 1960), while the volume of imports jumped by eleven per cent and their value by thirteen per cent.

The Netherlands alone amongst the Six showed an actual drop in production during the greater part of 1961. However real the labour shortage, it is by itself not an explanation of this fact, though it is undoubtedly a brake on the rate of expansion. This may be a mere cooling-off, a pause to permit an overheated economy to recover its threatened balance in order to continue its long-term advance at a more leisurely pace. It may, however, also be a pointer towards the effect which a slackening of German economic growth is likely to have on the economy of neighbouring countries in proportion to their dependence on Germany as a market and as a supplier.

Perhaps the Dutch economy is a barometer for the reaction of all the members of the Six to the impulses emanating from its economic power centre, the German economy; it has been set 'fair' for a remarkably long period, but the Dutch experience suggests that it may be in the process of veering towards 'unsettled'; the possibility that one day it may turn towards 'stormy' cannot be completely ignored in a realistic assessment of future prospects.

Belgium

Among the Six, Belgium has the invidious distinction of being the country with the slowest rate of growth, far behind Germany and Italy and considerably behind France and the Netherlands. Its real gross product rose by 3.2 per cent per year between 1950 and 1955 and by only 2.4 per cent annually during the following five years. Industrial output expanded by twelve per cent between 1958 and 1960, but 1958 had been a depressed year and compared with 1956 or 1957 the advance was less than five per cent, with a modest improvement in manufacturing industry offsetting by a small margin the catastrophic decline in coal mining.

The crisis in the coal industry affected Belgium much more severely than its partners, for not only are many Belgium mines old and unproductive, but the share of coal mining in national output is much higher in Belgium. (In 1957 it was about four per cent compared with 2.5 per cent in Germany, 1.8 per cent in France and 1.6 per cent in the Netherlands.[12]) Despite the urgent demand for coal in the middle fifties, the low productivity of the Belgian mines was a source of embarrassment to the ECSC from the beginning, and the quick transition from shortage to glut in 1957/8 threw Belgium's plight into sharp relief. Coal production reached its peak in 1952/3 with over 2.5m. tons per month and declined slightly to 2.42m. by 1957; from then on output fell by over twenty per cent to 1.87m. per month in 1960 and 1.79m. tons in 1961.

[12] EEC, *Report*, etc. (1958), p. 226.

As a manufacturing country, Belgium traditionally specialized in iron and steel and mass production textile goods, both of them semi-finished products suitable for bulk trade but subject to wide fluctuations in demand, because they were mainly marginal supplies in export markets. Immediately after the war this policy paid high dividends, for there was an almost inexhaustible demand for coal, steel and textiles (not to mention copper and uranium from the Belgian Congo). During the later 1940s Belgium was an oasis of plenty and well-being in a Europe haunted by shortages and beset by rationing and controls. With a moderate political swing to the Left reinforcing the purely economic motives for a more generous wages policy, living conditions were easy, and Belgium's economic policy favoured *laissez faire* at home and maximum trade liberalization in international relations.

The same attitude dominated the Belgian system of public finance. The proportion of taxes consisting of direct taxation was remarkably small for an advanced country, and taxation as a whole was so low that regular public loans were needed to balance the budget; the cost of servicing the national debt thus rose from year to year and perpetuated the need for more loans. As the 'ceiling' for advances from the National Bank to the government was settled by law at a relatively low figure, public loans took the form of long-term bonds which accounted for more than three-quarters of all new issues. This may have contributed to the low level of real asset formation compared with Germany or the Netherlands which was characteristic of the Belgian economy since the war, though fairly energetic attempts are now being undertaken to increase it.

Crisis in coal mining, slow industrial growth and even the permanent deficit in the public household might have been contained within the traditional system without the intervention of two external factors: these were the creation of the EEC and the rude shock of the Congo disaster. Trade with the Congo was less important for Belgian exports than for imports of valuable materials which made it a pillar in Belgium's balance of payments. During the years preceding the ill-prepared grant of independence, this trade declined and capital was being repatriated, but the crisis of July, 1960, high-lighted the bankruptcy of Belgium's economic policy no less than that of its colonial administration and for a time threatened even the stability of the currency.

The influence of the Common Market was evident in the measures by which the discredited government attempted to solve its difficulties by a fairly severe deflationary policy *à la* Pinay. The result was an explosion which took it no less by surprise than the Socialist opposition. Though triggered-off by the events of the immediate past, it was in the main a reaction of the working class in the Walloon areas against pressures which had been building up for years. The strikes of December, 1960, and January, 1961, temporarily halted the economy (particularly the coal and steel areas of French-speaking Belgium) without doing permanent harm to production. Their most characteristic result was, however, political. It had been freely prophesied by the 'responsible' press that the impending general elections would lead to a defeat of the Socialists who were popularly, and much against the wishes of their moderate leaders, identified with the strikers; in fact the elections resulted in a swing to the Left and the replacement of the ruling Christian Social-Liberal coalition by a Christian Social-Socialist coalition government.

In trade relations Belgium had always been orientated towards its three neighbours, the Netherlands, Western Germany and France. Even in the early 1950s the EEC countries accounted for two-fifths of Belgian imports and over a third of Belgian exports, with the Netherlands in the lead both as a supplier and as a market. In the year of the Treaty of Rome the Community supplied 43.5 per cent of all imports and bought over forty-six per cent of Belgium's exports, and by 1961 these proportions had risen to more than half. The Netherlands remained by far the most important market, with Germany in second place, while Germany had become Belgium's biggest supplier even before the establishment of the Common Market. In 1961, a year of still buoyant foreign demand, sales to third countries actually declined while exports to the EEC rose by nine per cent. However, more recently German demand for Belgian steel has declined—another pointer indicating a temporary saturation of the demand for Belgium's prime export and a disturbing portent —while trade with France and the Netherlands has increased.

Belgium remains a very prosperous country, but its economic position has seriously deteriorated during the later 1950s and

F

its stagnation and relative decline has been in no way halted by its entry into the EEC. There may have been some fortuitous misfortunes, such as the reversal of the coal boom and the Congo crisis, but Belgium's share in the great trade and investment advance of 1959-61 has been disappointingly small. Such as it was, it was largely a by-product of over-full employment in Germany and Holland. This may be well in line with Belgium's traditional reliance on semi-finished manufactures, but merely to be called in as sub-contractor for the booming industry of its neighbours and to be dismissed when the boom has run its course is a precarious base for the future, even with the help of an occasional windfall such as the temporary boost to Belgian exports from the revaluation of Mark and Guilder.

Only the future can tell whether a radical improvement will result from the newly-found enthusiasm of the Belgian authorities for economic planning which produced the laws of July, 1959, for the encouragement of economic expansion and the use of a Five Year Plan on the French model with the aim of raising the increase in national production to the respectable level of four per cent per year, the elimination of structural unemployment and the modernization of industry. One thing, however, is clear for all to see: the failure of the official *laissez faire* policy (outside agriculture and, perhaps, transport) which led to stagnation at home and disaster abroad. Within the environment of the Common Market, to atone for these failures for deflation may have appeared as the only thing to do, but with a different balance of social and political forces from that in France it produced social conflict of an intensity which threatened the cohesion of the State and boomeranged on its originators.

Bearing in mind the experience of Belgium's coal industry in the ECSC it is open to doubt whether the EEC will favour a more successful approach to the problem of Belgium's antiquated industrial structure. A state of permanent boom would, indeed, provide an ideal climate for Belgian industry, and so far conditions have been more favourable than the greatest optimists would have thought possible. This has enabled Belgium to stave off drastic reforms, but an end to the boom, and still more the onset of a depression, might expose its industry to the full blast of superior competition in its home market and in that of its three neighbours on which it is almost equally dependent.

A country in Belgium's position and within the framework of the Common Market is, therefore, likely to be more planned against than planning, however important a purposive planning policy may be for a solution of its pressing problems.

Luxembourg

The separate existence of the Grand Duchy of Luxembourg is an accident, delightful for the tourist but incompatible with independent economic life, and since 1922 it has been in close economic union with Belgium. Its most important economic asset is the iron and steel industry in the extreme South which accounts for three-quarters of the country's industrial net output and for almost nine-tenths of its exports.

The economy which has grown around the steel industry is of mainly parochial importance, and some of it may not find the Common Market profitable or even painless. (Agriculture is protected by a special protocol to the Rome Treaty.) Although happily free from the troubles of coal mining, Luxembourg's economic future is inseparable from that of the steel industry and for this reason it will probably move more or less in step with Belgium.

(3) THE ECONOMIC EFFECTS OF INTEGRATION

The preceding outline of production and trading trends in the industrial sectors of the Community and in each of the Member States provides some raw material for an analysis of the preliminary economic results of the Common Market during the first four years of its existence. (As it can hardly be said to be as yet in operation in agriculture, transport and other fields, no attempt has been made to include them in this survey.)

The question of the economic effects of the EEC has been the subject of such grotesque partisan exaggeration that it must be answered in detail, even at the risk of stating the obvious in some respects and of having to rely on inadequate material in others. In addition, if all study of the past is in a way concerned with the present and, perhaps, even with the future, this practical concern is almost paramount in such a topical subject, and the problem of what economic integration has done for the Six during the past four years is inseparable from the issue of what it may do in the years ahead for them and the candidate-members of the new grouping.

Germany's Commanding Lead

Whatever else the EEC may have done, one thing is clear: during 1958-61 the differences in the rate of development between the Member States have not become smaller but have increased even further. The slowing-down in the rate of economic growth in France during 1959 was largely brought about by a deflationary policy directly related to the introduction of the new regime, while Belgium's chronic stagnation has not been cured by the more intimate contact with more dynamic countries. Above all, Germany's economic predominance vis-à-vis the rest has become even more marked than it was before. A convenient, if inaccurate, measure of this continuing shift can be obtained by applying the change in output indices since 1953 to the weighting adopted at the time for individual countries.

Table VII

Percentage share of EEC countries in industrial output

	1953	1957	1961
W. Germany	40.9	42.9	43.8
France	27.7	27.5	26.1
Italy	16.2	16.0	17.9
Netherlands	6.8	6.2	6.0
Belgium	7.9	6.9	5.8
Luxembourg	0.5	0.5	0.4
Total	100.0	100.0	100.0

calculated from OECD—*General Statistics*
Saar included in France 1953 and 1957 (1.0 per cent)
and in Germany in 1961 (0.8)

The share of Germany in the combined industrial output of the Six climbed from 1953 to 1957 and slightly improved during the following four years, even ignoring the acquisition of the Saar. France declined marginally between 1953 and 1957 and much more sharply since, partly due to the loss of the Saar and partly owing to a slowing down of its rate of growth. Italy slightly lost ground between 1953 and 1957 but increased fairly spectacularly in more recent years. The Netherlands relatively lost substantial ground between 1953 and 1957 and more gradually since then, while Belgium's share has fallen sharply and without interruption.

Another aspect of Germany's commanding place in the grouping is emphasized by the trade figures. The main difference between Germany and the other EEC countries during the period 1957 to 1960 lay in the fact that German exports rose almost equally to the Six and to the outside world, while the other five countries exported more and more to Germany whose imports from them rose between 1957 and 1960 by seventy-one per cent compared with sixty-eight per cent for Italy (on a very much smaller total), forty-one per cent for France, twenty-eight per cent for Belgium and twenty-three per cent for the Netherlands. In 1957, German imports from the EEC were valued at $1,763m., or just over one-eighth of the combined exports of the five countries; in 1960 they accounted for $3,010 or almost one-sixth of a much larger total; in 1961, this proportion rose further to $17\frac{1}{2}$ per cent. German exports to the EEC rose from $2,503m. (=29.2 per cent of German exports) in 1957 to $3,362 (=29.4 per cent) in 1960 and $4,027m. or 31.7 per cent in 1961—the first significant proportionate rise over the pre-EEC period.

The main cause of this partial 'anomaly' was Germany's supreme performance as an exporter of equipment goods (machinery of all kinds, including transport equipment) to the world at large. In this central branch of modern industry Germany is, of course, the undisputed leader amongst the Six and in 1960 about fifty-eight per cent of the combined equipment exports of the EEC came from Germany, or almost the same proportion as at the beginning of the boom. A substantial part of the flourishing equipment exports of the other Five went, in fact, to Germany; this may express a measure of specialization noted in connection with the relations between Germany and the Benelux countries which were feeding Germany's overextended engineering industries and thereby helped to satisfy the voracious world appetite for their products. Though Benelux was the most important sub-contractor for German industry within the Community, the overspill of the German boom into neighbouring countries was just as evident in the case of Austria, with a high proportion of exports going to Germany, a sizeable number of border-crossing workers and increasing numbers of German firms establishing branch factories on Austrian soil.

'Discrimination' and Trade

The German example also helps to establish another negative fact about the first four years of the Common Market. This is the very limited importance of preferences in duties on manufactures, at least during a time of very active business conditions. German duties had been cut unilaterally in August, 1957, by 20-25 per cent for a wide range of manufactured goods imported from all sources. In these cases no preference was established for the Six before January, 1961, and then only on a very modest scale. Nevertheless, German imports of equipment goods from the EEC more than trebled in value between 1957 and 1960 and imports of other manufactures almost doubled, showing in both cases much higher rates of increase than imports from other sources (as well as higher rates than those achieved by the other Member States from any source). The experience of the rest of the Community suggests, plausibly enough, a rather stronger response to duty changes in the high-tariff countries France and Italy than in low-tariff Benelux, and these differences will no doubt be studied at leisure by specialists in international trade.

On the whole, the reduction in intra-Community duties seems to have been relatively most effective in primary commodities, where total imports rose much less and where the diversion of trade from third countries to the Community is at first sight very striking.

It has been argued persuasively[13] that the increase in trade between the EEC countries since the formation of the Community is merely the continuation of long-term trends which were not substantially changed by this event. The facts do not support this claim in the case of primary commodities, while the position for manufacturers is considerably more complex. The following table gives some indication of the changes which have occurred year by year in the value of trade in the main commodity groups, both in exchanges amongst the Six and in their imports from third countries.

[13] By M. Lamfalussy in *Lloyds Bank Review*, October, 1961.

Table VIII

EEC imports from Member States and third Countries
(annual percentage change by value)

	Food, Drink, Tobacco	Raw Materials	Fuel	Equipment	Other Manuf.	Total
(i) from Members						
average 1953-7	14.1	10.5	9.1	20.1	17.4	15.6
1958 over 57	6.9	—17.7	—5.3	2.4	—1.7	—3.5
1959 over 58	23.9	27.7	0.4	17.0	21.7	19.2
1960 over 59	15.3	25.4	11.8	26.5	31.4	25.4
average 1957-60	10.0	9.6	2.1	14.9	16.2	13.0
(ii) from third Countries						
average 1953-57	8.2	10.7	9.2	12.5	16.7	12.8
1958 over 1957	1.1	—20.4	—14.2	—3.7	1.1	—9.2
1959 over 1958	—1.2	—1.0	—11.2	1.6	15.7	0.7
1960 over 1959	5.3	24.5	8.5	44.4	29.2	20.2
average 1957-60	2.1	—0.6	—6.1	12.2	15.7	3.1

Though less crude than the point-to-point comparisons in Table IV, these figures tell essentially the same story, though with some significant additions. Compared with the period 1953-7, the shift towards intra-Community trade in food, drink and tobacco has been greatly speeded up; during the earlier period intra-Community trade increased rather less than twice as fast as imports from third countries; during 1957-60 the increase was five times as much. Raw material trade during 1953-57 increased in value at a surprisingly even rate for all sources, and the fall in 1958 also affected them roughly to the same extent; however, in 1959 intra-Community trade rose by a quarter while exports from third countries continued to drop slightly, and although the expansion in 1960 was very similar for all sources compared with 1959 this barely enabled third countries to approach the 1957 level, while intra-Community trade expanded on average during the period 1957-60 almost as much as during the preceding four years. The diversion of trade is even more striking in the case of fuel, because the market as a whole showed little change in total value, if the post-Suez peak in 1957 is ignored, though the relatively small proportion of intra-Community trade makes detailed comparisons of growth rates unprofitable.

For manufactured goods there is much less uniformity. At first sight, the intra-Community trade in equipment has fared relatively worse than imports from third countries. In 1953-57 it expanded considerably more quickly than such imports, during 1957-60 the average rates of growth were almost the same; closer inspection suggests, however, that the excellent showing of imports from third countries was limited to 1960 and may therefore have been mainly due to the full use of Community resources; if this is true, it may, therefore, be a very temporary feature. For other manufactures the rate of growth was by and large the same for members and outsiders, though more detailed analysis might unearth considerable differences between the many different industries lumped together in this group.

The Stimulus to Investment

Perhaps the most definite strictly economic effect of the Treaty of Rome has been its influence on the volume of investment. As the great boom of 1959-61 was in the first place an investment boom, this means that the establishment of the Common Market had at least some share in creating the very favourable economic climate which, more than anything else, assisted the progress of the Community during its earliest years. Assured of a favourable environment, business men were content to plan ahead on the basis of expanding markets and rising profits.

In many cases their plans took the form of closer co-operation with related or competing firms in other member countries, either through the exchange of marketing facilities or through specialization of products or processes which results almost by definition in a significant increase in fixed investment. In addition, the initial success of the Common Market was the signal for a veritable flood of mergers which shows little sign of abating. Such mergers were frequently carried out within single countries as a means of strengthening the competitive strength of national industries in the new environment, particularly in France with its multitudes of small and medium-sized enterprises. However, a large and growing number of such arrangements extended to more than one Community country, as a kind of institutional parallel to the blossoming of trade associations amongst the Six. In an era of economic growth, such mergers were less an occasion for the closing down of less efficient units in order to weed out excess capacity than an opportunity for overall rationalization and for the expansion of the most efficient plants—or for the construction of new ones through further capital investment.

A small but significant contribution to the upsurge of investment was provided directly by the Community's new investment funds, the European Investment Bank and the European Development Fund for associated overseas territories. In 1960-1, the Bank approved eight financing operations in Italy, France and West Berlin; although the credits granted amounted to only 68m. 'units of account' (equal to the U.S. dollar), the total investment involved in these projects was over 469m. 'units'.[14] The overseas projects approved by the Development Fund reached about 250m. 'units' by the end of 1961.

Even more important was the injection of foreign capital in the industry of the Six, particularly from American sources. Before the birth of the EEC, the most popular American choice for long-term capital investment in Europe had been Britain, because it presented hardly any language problems and was the ideal jumping-off ground for Commonwealth trade, particularly in industries benefiting from Imperial Preference.

Despite the old American belief that the Commonwealth held out the best opportunities for American trade expansion, this motive lost much of its strength with the decline of Imperial Preference and the loosening of the economic ties between Britain and the Commonwealth, while the failure of Britain's Free Trade Area concept threatened British branches of American firms with exclusion from the fast-growing European market. The emphasis on the direction of American overseas investment towards Britain consequently changed and the Six soon began to overtake Britain. In 1960 they accounted for $436m. of new U.S. capital compared with $367m. in Britain (apart from the $350m. spent by Ford on acquiring the minority interests of British shareholders). Between 1958 and 1961, the Common Market countries received five American investment projects for every one going to Britain. Nevertheless, at the end of 1959 American direct investments in the United Kingdom at $2,475m. were higher than in the EEC as a whole ($2,194m.) and more than three times the figure for Germany which had the largest—and most profitable—share of American investment amongst the Six.[15]

---

[14] *Fourth General Report*, para. 101.
[15] E. Benoit, *Europe at Sixes and Sevens* (1961), p. 194.

With the exception of Germany, where there is growing hostility towards foreign ownership of important industries, the Six vied with each other in attracting dollar investment, and the range of American firms going into Europe widened from year to year, with engineering and chemicals still in the lead but with a steadily growing number of consumer goods manufacturers establishing branches. The largest number of American projects was secured by the Benelux countries (202), with the big three sharing about equally in the rest (France—145, Italy 135 and Germany—126).[16] Perhaps the most remarkable feature is the large contingent of firms favouring Italy which a few years ago would have been regarded as most unpromising ground for such ventures, but which now attracts American firms of the standing of US Steel and Westinghouse, not to mention the growing number of investors from the other member countries of the EEC. This makes, however, good commercial sense, for the profits of 12.6 per cent on capital (after tax) earned on American investments in Italy in 1958-9, though well below the astronomical 20.1 per cent achieved in Western Germany, were about half as high again as in the other Common Market countries.[17]

In addition to the factors mentioned before, and inseparable from most of then, a first-rate influence on the volume of investment in the Six has been the official policy of encouraging capital investment, both foreign and domestic, which is not really dependent on the existence of the Community. With the partial exception of Germany, where emphasis on investment pervades the whole economic system and special inducements are therefore less necessary, most of the Six offer extremely attractive conditions for such investment in the shape of direct assistance, loans on favourable terms and far-reaching tax benefits which make such a policy exceptionally profitable.

The Community and Economic Policy

It has been noted before that the economic principles of the Rome Treaty are an extension of the aspirations of Germany's 'social market economy' to the Six. These may be summed up as free play for the forces of free enterprise with partial compensation for the more important interests adversely affected by

16 Reported in *The Times*, October 24, 1961.
17 Benoit, *op. cit.*, p. 195.

its operation and with a special regime for agriculture. There is a strong emphasis on capital formation 'through the price', i.e. through high profit margins which permit the ploughing back of large sums into profitable undertakings, with wage increases limited to proportions justified by higher productivity and without encroaching on profits.

Although the theoretical justification of the 'market' aspect of the system is the maintenance of free competition, this ostensible framework is in practice modified, or even nullified, by ample opportunities for mergers and even for cartels. In fact, one of the hopeful forecasts generally made by economists about the consequences of the Common Market has so far been realized at the expense of the other. It has certainly provided an effective stimulus for capital investment, but not on the basis of free competition. On the contrary, all the available evidence points to a growing concentration of economic power as a result of the new business opportunities provided by the Community which the half-hearted anti-cartel rules of the EEC are unlikely to affect very much, particularly because old-fashioned cartels are much less important in this context than monopolies and near-monopolies on which the Treaty has even less to say than on cartels. The hopeful equation of 'more investment plus competition=more welfare, is, therefore, vitiated in practice in a vital particular.

If the essential discipline of competition is missing for business, the existence of the Common Market has carried out a discipline of a different kind in the pervasive pressure of its prospects as well as its actual operation on the economic policy of those of its members which were not already conforming to it. This fact is of such transcendent importance that it cannot be overemphasized, as its future application to new entrants to the Community would almost inevitably follow from what has already happened in the two instructive instances of France and Belgium.

The wholesale adoption of the principles of the social market economy by France at the eve of the first duty and quota changes in January, 1959, was without a doubt the most spectacular assertion of this Common Market 'discipline'. The political basis of this change, the establishment of the authoritarian and bureaucratic Fifth Republic, had no visible connection with the Treaty of Rome, but the economic policy adopted by the new regime cannot be separated from it: '. . . it is quite clear that entry into the Common Market was the essential motivating force for the draconian measures taken at the end of 1958. Had this prospect not existed, the leaders of France would have been justified in not trying to go so far with their reforms—which public opinion would in any case have accepted less willingly. It is certain that the success of the measures taken could not have been so great, had France not been a member of the Economic Community, with all its effects on the structure of the economy.'[18]

The events of 1960-61 in Belgium are scarcely less significant, for the pressure of Common Market orthodoxy was clearly evident in the 'loi unique' which exploded the accumulated tensions of Belgian society. The subordination of investment to consumption and the high wage levels characteristic of postwar Belgium may have been less a matter of free and deliberate choice than a semi-automatic response to short-term conditions, and when changed circumstances and the close integration with more dynamic countries exposed the system to increasingly severe strains, the official reaction followed almost inevitably the pattern of deflation and attacks on real wages.

Within an expanding economy or, in order not to beg an important and possibly decisive question, on the upswing of the trade cycle such a policy, however painful at the moment, may for a certain time delay growth and reduce living standards, but it can be defended as a necessary attempt to change the rules of the game in favour of a temporarily handicapped national economy. It may be represented fairly plausibly as a case of *reculer pour mieux sauter*, even though the cost of the process is normally thrown on the shoulders of those least able to bear it, while the benefits of the ensuing advance accrue in the first place to big business. This was the way in which Common Market discipline operated in fact in France and, at least in the intention of its authors, in Belguim: it was a clear-cut attempt to change the division of the national income by a 'pause' in the rise in wages (or a decline in real wages) and other incomes under the complete or partial control of the authorities, coupled with measures for making business more profitable.

As the Common Market has so far not supplied any justifica-

[18] V. G. d'Estaing (at the time French State Secretary for Finance, now Minister of Finance) in *The Financial Times*, November 27, 1961.

tion for the belief that its operation will tend to reduce the uneven pace in the development of its national constituents, such tension in the more slowly advancing countries is bound to arise even in times of economic expansion. So far there has not been time enough to experience the effects of such discrepancies in a period of declining trade or even, however heretical the very mention of the word, in a contracting economy. In this context, the experience of the two French-speaking member countries of the Community may well be of great symptomatic importance, with the fateful difference that in such a case deflationary pressures would not be balanced but intensified by the prevailing economic trend, and instead of resulting in a mere 'pause' in economic advance, might well cause an intensification of a deflationary spiral.

It is thus more than a coincidence that painful adjustments in policy were demanded by the Common Market even in a period of expansion from the countries whose rates of economic growth were lower than those of the leaders. If this balance continues, the Common Market would inevitably become a radically destabilizing influence in a period of declining trade.

III

THE FORCE OF GRAVITY

(1) THE OVERSEAS ASSOCIATES

The developing relationship between the Community and the 'associated overseas countries and territories' is a remarkable illustration of its flexibility and growth potential. It started as little more than just another French claim for exceptional treatment at a fairly late stage in the negotiations, at the Venice Conference of May, 1956, and at the time the main purpose of the exercise seemed to be the shift of part of the heavy burden of colonial capital expenditure from the finances of France to those of its more solvent but unwilling partners.

The Treaty provided for the abolition of duties on imports from the overseas associates by the Six and for the extension to all Community States of the preferences granted by the associates to their metropolitan countries (art. 133). However, the Six and particularly Germany showed a definite lack of enthusiasm for having to foot a large part of the bill even on these terms, and the first Implementing Convention was therefore limited to five years until the end of 1962, leaving the decision on further measures to the Council (art. 136). Despite this limitation, the amounts involved were quite large, for the income of the Development Fund set up at the same time was fixed at \$581¼m. for the five year period, to be financed by \$200m. each from France and Germany, \$70m. each from Belgium and the Netherlands, with \$40m. from Italy and the one and a quarter million dollars from Luxembourg. Of the benefits, no less than \$511¼m. was earmarked for the associated French colonies, \$35m. for the Netherlands, \$30m. for Belgium and \$5m. for Italian Somaliland.

Long before the natural end of the Convention the political links between France and almost all the African territories which formed the bulk of the associates had been severed, and the same fate had befallen the Italian trusteeship over Somaliland and Belgian rule in the Congo. However, the hostility of the ex-colonial African States towards colonialism generally did not extend to the economic links between them and the EEC, although their cash benefits from the Development Fund during the first four financial years had been less than one-half of the amount allocated for the five year period. In addition, some of the advantages to which they became entitled in the form of duty reductions on tropical products were, in effect, cancelled by the action of some of the Six which either cut duties but simultaneously increased excise taxes, or, as was the case with coffee in Western Germany, reduced import duties from all sources to the level of the common external tariff and thus deprived the associates of their preferential position compared with the Latin American buyers of German manufactures.

The activities of the Development Fund improved steadily, partly spurred by criticism from the associates of its cumbersome procedure. As the change from colonial status to independence weakened at the same time the claims of the associated States on the resources of the old colonial powers, the Fund was bound to assume growing importance. Early in 1961 applications for finance had reached a total of $670m., fifteen per cent in excess of its total income for the first five years.[1] The technical problems of preparing and processing assistance projects were complicated by the need for direct contacts with the newly independent States while previously transactions were channelled through the European Member States. The Commission tried to cope with the resulting congestion by temporary missions on the spot which could discuss, and if possible approve, applications from each State en bloc.[2]

Even more important than the refashioning of economic procedures was the adaptation of political relations to the new situation. For this purpose the community employed in the first place the European Parliament as a suitable link with the emerging nations. A preliminary meeting between parliamentarians of the Six and of the African States (including Madagascar), attended by representatives of the Commission, took place in

[1] Fourth General Report, para. 168.   [2] ibid., para. 171.

Rome in January, 1961. It had the task of preparing for a full-scale parliamentary Conference in Strasbourg which was held in June-July, 1961, and which laid the basis for the negotiations between the EEC Council and the governments of the associated States through a series of resolutions which were, of course, legally only 'recommendations'.

The inevitable starting point of the new relationship was a recognition of the sovereign equality of all parties to it, and the unanimous agreement to retain the association between the EEC and the new States in order 'to promote the economic and social development of the associated States and to establish close economic relations between them and the European Community with the primary aim of furthering the interests and prosperity of the inhabitants of these States in such a manner as to lead them to the economic, social and cultural development which they expect'.[3] The terms of this association are to take the form of a model convention which will be entered into separately by the EEC and each State. The new institutions are to consist of a parliamentary conference, a Council of Association and an Arbitration Court.

In the economic field, the Conference recommended measures to increase trade between the associated States and the EEC and to further their economic development and planning by a whole series of steps, including help from Euratom, the commitment of the whole European Development Fund resources before the end of 1962 and its replacement by a Common Development Fund. In the cultural field the existing training schemes were to be continued and extended, both in respect of general education (including scholarships) and technical and vocational training.

One of the most important features of the Conference, with potentially ominous implications, was the emphatic insistence on the maintenance of a preferential relationship between the Community and the Associates. Politically this emerged most clearly from the sixth recommendation 'that the new association, which will not be limited to a specific term, should be open to all African States, subject to the proviso that none of them may belong to another economic grouping which pursues ends incompatible with those of the association'. (*ibid.*) The future was soon to show that this clause was partly directed against the African members of the Commonwealth, but its main purpose

[3] EEC *Bulletin*, July-August, 1961, p. 133.

was to prevent any attempt at combined membership of both organizations. Thus it formed part of the Community's general strategic approach to Britain.

On the economic side the demands of the associated States on the Six were resolutely protectionist for themselves and therefore rather less convenient for countries relying heavily on the taxation of tropical foods and beverages, and particularly for Germany and the Netherlands with their far-flung trade interests. The Conference endorsed the African claim for 'the abolition, without delay, of . . . internal consumer taxes on tropical products' which 'have whittled away the tariff advantages which the Treaty intended that the associated States should enjoy'.[4] It also demanded in connection with the common external tariff that 'care must be taken to see that the tariff preference margins are strictly maintained', that no new duty-free import quotas are granted, 'that the associated States should be the first to benefit from any increase in consumption' and that special measures should be taken for the stabilization of prices and quantities of the tropical products concerned.

The Commission viewed this emphasis on the exclusive and preferential character of the proposed association with some concern, specially in view of the unconcealed American hostility towards the whole concept and its particularly serious effects on Latin America. Its own plan, published in the autumn of 1961, wished to guarantee to the Associated States 'a series of advantages at least equivalent to those they enjoyed at the time of their association with the EEC',[5] but to concentrate less on protective measures than on price stability and development help.

This policy would involve a many-pronged approach to the problem. Thus the Commission proposed to move away from the guaranteed quotas for certain African staple products in the French market, but to cut back at the same time the large duty-free quotas for imports of coffee into Italy and Benelux and of bananas into Germany, while abolishing consumer taxes on coffee and cocoa in two steps by the beginning of 1965 and reducing the tariff rates on these products. In addition, 'anti-cyclical' loans, direct production aid for tropical products (in the first place coffee, bananas and cotton) and a joint Production Fund of $25m. a year were proposed as well as EEC partici-

[4] ibid., p. 135
[5] EEC Bulletin, September-October, 1961, pp. 31ff.

G

pation in international price stabilization agreements.

The new Common Development Fund would dispose of $220m. a year as against the European Development Fund's $116m. but as it should make loans as well as grants, the effective burden on the Member States would remain roughly unchanged, and greater emphasis would be put on encouraging private investment. Although continuity in the operations of the new institutions was essential, the new Implementing Convention should be limited to a period of seven years in the interests of greater flexibility.

The conflicting demands for preferential treatment by the Associated States and outside pressure against discrimination affecting third parties were much in evidence during the negotiations in the autumn and winter of 1961-2. Its culmination was a Ministerial Conference between the Six and their Associates in December, 1961, which ended inconclusively. A compromise about half-way between the *status quo* and the Commission's proposals was elaborated by the Six in June, 1962, and a new system will come into force on January 1, 1963.

Within the Community, Germany (supported by the Netherlands) is said to have favoured the complete abolition of the tariff preferences on tropical products in exchange for financial compensation to the African States; France (with the support of Belgium) is said to have argued, on the contrary, that the *status quo* with its preferences for the associated States should be maintained. The African States themselves appear to have left no doubt about the importance which they attributed to preferential treatment over outsiders as well as over latecomers to the Community. This claim of the (mainly ex-French) Associates for special privileges over possible Commonwealth candidates for membership is bound to increase the distrust of the Common Market expressed by a number of African Commonwealth countries and their reluctance to consider association on any terms, not to mention on worse terms than those of the present Associates.

The principle of association between the Six and their overseas territories thus tended to outlive the colonial relationship on which it was originally based and even assumed an impetus of its own, but this may well introduce in the longer term a new disruptive element into the delicate relations between the backward countries as a whole and the advanced capitalist nations of the West.

In the meantime, the outstanding fact is the substantial economic attraction for the underdeveloped areas concerned of cultivating close links with the most dynamic grouping of rich countries in the world. This has also induced the cautious Dutch to take up their 'option' to associate Surinam with the EEC and to make similar arrangements for the Dutch Antilles. The latter request ran into difficulties owing to French opposition, because it raised in acute form the problem of how oil products refined within the Community from foreign oil should be treated under the common external tariff. While France was most directly concerned about competition for oil from the Sahara, the possibility of Italian refineries using oil from the Middle East or from politically tainted Eastern sources could hardly be completely ignored.

The agreement reached in November, 1961, after very lengthy negotiations accepted the Dutch Antilles as an associated territory but limited imports of oil products on preferential terms to two million tons per year, subject to special 'peril point' provisions for the Community as a whole as well as for each of the importing member countries. This follows similar compromise arrangements in the agreement with Greece and was apparently accepted by the Dutch only with great reluctance. The device is potentially of considerable importance, and quotas for preferential imports from associated territories might well play a prominent part in the negotiations on Commonwealth imports.

(2) 'GOOD NEIGHBOUR' AND 'BIG STICK'

The countries of Southern Europe, like the Italian South, are essentially backward peasant economies with rudimentary industries and stunted agricultural systems. Their foreign trade is on a much lower level than that of the EEC members and their exports consist largely of a few staple products such as fruit, fish, wine, tobacco or cotton. They are therefore very vulnerable to pressure from more advanced trading partners willing to take their exports but on terms appealing to the buyer, a state of affairs exemplified in extreme form by Germany's trading policy in the Balkans during the 1930s. The formation of the EEC, which in Italy includes at least one country directly competing with them in some of their few important export products, was therefore a challenge and a threat, particularly in view of the fact that the proposed common agricultural policy was from the start frankly protectionist in aim and at least potentially autarkic in effect.

At the same time, the comprehensive character of the Treaty of Rome, its flexibility and the recognition of the obligations of advanced countries to contribute towards the development of poorer regions, held out some promise of helping these countries in solving their pressing problems. It would be far too dangerous for them to remain outside the alternative trade blocks in Europe, and Britain's original counter-plan of a European Free Trade area excluding agriculture, as well as its partial realization in the European Free Trade Association ('Efta'), was totally lacking in features attractive, or even tolerable, to them, although it included in Portugal at least nominally one inhabitant of the European agricultural slum. For this reason the two relatively uncommitted backward countries of South Eastern Europe, Greece and Turkey, soon stretched out feelers for a possible accommodation with the EEC.

The first request for an association with the Common Market was made by the Greek government in June, 1959, and a draft agreement embodying the terms of the arrangement was signed at the end of March, 1961. The EEC Council of Ministers gave its approval on June 12th and the Treaty was signed in Athens on July 9, 1961, in breach of art. 238 of the Treaty of Rome which stipulates that the Council shall act in such a case 'after consulting the Assembly'. The fact that it was not submitted to the European Parliament until after signature may well represent part of the jockeying for position in connection with the impending British application for membership rather than a gratuitous slight to the Parliament by the Council.

The duration of the negotiations was not only the result of their pioneering character but also of the special problems of the case. On the one hand, Greece needed more protection for its infant industries than the members of the EEC, on the other hand some of Greece's few exports (citrus fruit, olive oil and wine) are competitive with Italy's. These difficulties were intensified by the lack of an agreed common agricultural policy for the Six which made it almost impossible to anticipate how Greek trade would fit into the future framework of agricultural trade. In these circumstances there could be no question of a straightforward extension of the Rome Treaty to Greece, nor of the application of its fourth part dealing with the association of the overseas territories, although great efforts were made to demonstrate how flexible the Treaty of Rome was in practice.

In principle it has been agreed to set up a customs union between the EEC and Greece applying immediately to imports from Greece the rates of duty applied to Member States—in view of the negligible volume of Greek industrial exports a mere flourish and not a genuine concession. On the other hand, Greece will be allowed to spread the abolition of duties on about one-third of its imports from the EEC over twenty-two years; on these goods, duties will be cut by only one-fifth during the first ten years and the balance will be removed according to the time table of the Rome Treaty for the period of transition. During the first twelve years of the agreement, Greece will also be allowed temporarily to raise tariffs on imports from the Community for the protection of its infant industries.

Greece by and large accepted the common external tariff of the Community, but certain exceptions have been agreed in favour of some imports from third countries and special tariff quotas have been permitted for supplies from the United States connected with the use of American aid. The complicated rules for agricultural trade try to make room for larger Greek exports of some products (such as tobacco and raisins) to the Six, while preventing embarrassing competition of Greek fruit and wine with Italy.

In order to help in the adjustment of the Greek economy to growing competition from its new partners, Greece will receive a development loan of $125m. from the Community during the first five years. Some common policies will be extended to Greece, usually after a considerable time lag. Thus the free movement of workers (which is particularly valuable for Greece with its widespread underemployment of rural labour) will be introduced 'at the earliest on the expiry of the twelve-year transition period'; an attempt by the Socialist members of the European Parliament to write into the Agreement assurances about the freedom of Greek Trade Unions was defeated.

On the other hand, the Community has characteristically laid special value on the speedy extension of the 'right of establishment' to Greece; this does not mean that there is any eagerness on the part of German or French doctors, lawyers, etc., to practise their professions in the shadow of the Acropolis but, in the words of the official EEC commentary, that 'this is a necessary condition if the influx of private capital is to be stimulated and guarantees are to be available that it can be invested without discrimination based on nationality'.[6]

This is a proviso of the greatest importance; given the enormous disparity in wealth and economic power between Greece and the Six, it introduces into their relations a potentially disastrous element of economic colonialism which is incompatible with healthy national development. To protect Greek industries for up to twenty-two years from direct competition by EEC manufactures, while creating the conditions for uncontrolled large-scale investment in Greece by financial and industrial interests of the Six, completely ignores the social and political consequences of such action in an underdeveloped peasant country. Against this background, the formal parity between Greece and the Community in the proposed Council of Association is little more than a sham.

As there is a certain discrepancy between the type of association embodied in the Agreement and the open invitation of art. 237 of the Rome Treaty to 'any European State' to apply for full membership, provision is made for the 'eventual accession of Greece to the EEC, should the Association Agreement work well enough to enable that country to contemplate full acceptance of the obligations deriving from the Treaty of Rome'.

The background to the negotiations was a developing serious threat to important Greek exports to the Six. In 1958, the EEC took well over forty per cent of Greek exports—$98m. out of a total of $232m.; by 1960 the proportion had fallen to one-third —$67m. out of $203m. Thus the fall in exports to the EEC countries was responsible for the great bulk of the decline in Greek exports as a whole; exports to the Efta countries increased marginally and those to Eastern Europe showed an irregularly rising trend, but this was not enough to compensate for the drop in exports to the Six which was particularly pronounced for beverages and tobacco exports, while the fall in food and raw materials has been rather less severe. (To some extent this was the result of unusually heavy French imports in 1958.) Thus it was the threat of the Community rather than its promise which

[6] EEC *Bulletin*, April, 1961, pp. 21f.

provided the ultimate guarantee for the success of the negotiations.

In the case of *Turkey*, which applied for association at about the same time as Greece, the export experience was more encouraging (except for tobacco), but the very fact that little progress was made while the talks with Greece were pushed through to a successful conclusion, by itself put Turkey under pressure. Only after the signature of the Association Agreement with Greece did the Council of EEC declare its intention to enter into negotiations, but no substantial progress had been made by the end of 1961.

Preliminary discussions with *Tunisia* on a similar agreement do not seem to have come to much, while negotiations with *Israel* are apparently in progress. The Israeli government has denied reports that its request for admission as a full member had been rejected or that it would be willing to consider full membership; it claimed that its only concern was the avoidance of discrimination against Israeli exports and regarded the Agreement between the Six and Greece as a possible model for its own relationship with the Community.[7] The devaluation of the Israeli pound by forty per cent in February, 1962, was officially described as a reform to meet the challenge of the Common Market.

In the extreme North West of Europe, the Government of the *Republic of Ireland* watched the development of the EEC with intense but ambivalent interest. After a generation of modestly successful efforts in building up a parochial and highly protected national industry, the threat of the complete removal of customs barriers was very distasteful to important vested interests; on the other hand, some of the more articulate spokesmen of the farmers clamoured for an approach to the Common Market, as the principles of the common agricultural policy promised near-miracles for Irish agriculture which in the past had been almost entirely dependent on the most depressed market for agricultural surpluses in the world, the United Kingdom. However, with Britain striking out in a different direction, the Irish government was in no position to make up its mind, for an association with the EEC to the exclusion of Britain would not have made economic sense. On the other hand, the British-sponsored Free Trade Association was of no possible in-

7 Reported in *The Times*, December 14, 1961.

terest to the Irish Republic, because it excluded agriculture. The country thus remained precariously perched at the edge of both rival groups.

As soon as it became evident in the first half of 1961 that Britain was veering towards the EEC, Ireland made a direct approach to the Six and informed them on July 4, 1961, of its intention of applying for full membership on certain conditions. This step may have been motivated by the double anxiety of preventing Ireland's isolation from the main stream of European integration and of avoiding the appearance of acting as a British satellite. In fact, the official Irish application for full membership was made on July 31, 1961, the very day on which the British Prime Minister announced in the House of Commons the decision to open negotiations and nine days before the British application was made.

Although at great pains to stress the independent nature of its initiative, the Irish government could not really be in any doubt about the inevitable order of priorities, because a decision on Ireland's application was obviously dependent on the prior settlement between Britain and the Community. The accession of a mainly agricultural country with a high growth potential in fields where the EEC as a whole was already in danger of over-supply would in any case present delicate problems; these were intensified by Ireland's original claim to special terms and by political doubts whether Ireland's abstention from NATO would be an obstacle to full Irish membership of the Community. Within the Council, the Irish application provoked a clash between its supporters, Germany and the Netherlands, and France and Italy who opposed it. After once adjourning the discussion, the Council gave a guarded reply at the end of October, 1961, which suggested an 'examination of the problems' early in 1962.

When this took place on January 18, 1962, it was mainly the occasion for a general statement by the Irish Prime Minister, Mr Sean Lemass, which virtually withdrew the demand for special treatment for Irish industries, though it included a plea for an appropriate rhythm of tariff reduction in the case of protective duties, and suggested the possibility of a protocol safeguarding 'some basically sound industries'. He also specifically emphasized Ireland's acceptance of the political aims of the Community, including the general aims of the NATO Treaty.

In keeping with the cautious approach of the Six, the discussions were then adjourned. Only a few weeks later, on February 9, 1962, the Spanish Government of General Franco applied for association with the EEC with a view to ultimate full membership.

Thus there can be no doubt about the powerful attraction of the Community for the smaller and poorer countries, nor about the fact that the common denominator in their attitude is not hope but fear. Its attraction for them is less the positive expectation of economic gain—though this does not, of course, prevent them from applying to the Six for credits and other help—but the need to avoid at all costs exclusion from a large and growing trading area. The consequences of the alternative are, however, plain. In the words of Mr Lemass, 'in the new situation we cannot hope to maintain sales either at home or abroad of any products unless they can meet the test of competitiveness of price. That is the hard inescapable fact which must henceforward govern every policy and every decision'.[8]

The understandable concern of these countries for the future reflects in the last resort the fact that the price they must pay for a largely negative advantage is to forswear 'national discrimination', or—to put it more bluntly—to abandon any independent economic policy of their own in favour of a social market economy designed to perpetuate the social and economic advantages of the strong at the expense of the weak.

(3) BRITAIN VERSUS THE SIX

Favoured by the course of events and propelled by the motive force of powerful economic interests, the EEC has managed to overcome its inevitable teething troubles and—sometimes— even to learn from the disagreements between its members, but at least some credit for its remarkable progress must go to the curiously inept policy of the British government during the crucial years since 1957.

Throughout 1957 and 1958, Britain clung obstinately to the concept of an exclusively industrial European Free Trade Area as its aim and to the many-headed OEEC negotiations as its

[8] Reported in *Bulletin of the Department of External Affairs*, Dublin, December 4, 1961.

method. The reception of the original plan should have made it clear to the British authorities that no agreement could be reached on this basis and that the crux of any agreement would have to be an understanding with France. It may have been obvious to the dispassionate observer that at the time France was in no position to widen the area of free foreign competition by including all the most advanced industrial nations of North Western Europe in a Free Trade Area without any of the compensating benefits of the Treaty of Rome; if this fundamental fact was understood in Britain, it remained without the slightest influence on the British negotiators whose tactics seemed to be modelled on those of the Allied generals on the Western Front during the first world war.

At present it cannot be known for certain whether this perverse approach helped to convert General de Gaulle to the merits of the European Economic Community, but its final upshot was clear for all to see in the amazing scene which buried the European Free Trade Area plan (and the OEEC) in the angry exchanges between the French Foreign Minister and the President of the Board of Trade in November, 1958. This was followed almost immediately by the abandonment of the European Payments Union which may or may not have had the purpose of forcing the hands of the French government but helped to bring about the further devaluation of the French franc and propelled France towards the policy of the social market economy and the German alliance.

Britain's reply to the failure of the 'big' European Free Trade Area was the 'little' European Free Trade Association of the Outer Seven—Britain, Denmark, Norway, Sweden, Austria, Switzerland and Portugal. The initiative to this step, and some of the urgency behind it, may have come from other countries and particularly from Sweden and Switzerland, but it could become practical politics only through the backing of the British government. The three Scandinavian members of the Seven (plus Finland) had made limited progress with the formation of a Nordic Common Market, but such a step, even if successful, would have been only of parochial importance. The accession of Switzerland and Austria, both almost surrounded by Common Market territory, expressed rather the political limitations on their freedom of action than any hopes of large economic gain, and the entry of Portugal into the new organization was recog-

nized as an empty gesture by the special conditions attached
to it.

The Soviet government again demonstrated its habitual
political myopia by preventing Finland from signing the Stockholm Agreement in November, 1959, as a founder member,
which might have given Russia an influence almost approaching a veto over the policy of Efta; when saner counsels prevailed
in the Kremlin, conditions had changed sufficiently to induce
Efta to exclude Finland's—and therefore Russia's—pocket veto
by creating a separate organization for co-operation with Finland rather than to accept it as a member of the original body.
(The pretext chosen for this sensible step unwittingly demolished one of the basic tenets behind the conception of a Free
Trade Area, the feasibility of excluding third-country products
by the device of certificates of origin; if this was a really effective
method, there would have been no good reason for treating
Finland differently from the rest because of its special economic
ties with the Soviet Union.)

The inherent weaknesses of Efta were partly due to the limitations of a Free Trade Area and partly a consequence of its composition. Like the original British plan it excluded agriculture
and formed an exclusive club incapable of finding room for the
economically forgotten backward countries. In addition, there
was from the start a gulf between those of its members for whom
it was an alternative to the Common Market, particularly the
neutrals Sweden and Switzerland, and those who regarded it
principally as a bridge with the EEC. This group included Denmark and the United Kingdom, with Norway in an intermediate position, while Austria belonged to it economically but
had to co-operate with the other neutrals for political reasons.

Denmark had joined Efta against the opposition of the powerful farming interests and largely for political reasons which
were underpinned by the special concessions to Danish agriculture made by Britain, Sweden and Switzerland as a condition
precedent to the Danish signature of the Stockholm Agreement.
However, within Efta Danish influence was immediately employed for the purpose of attacking its limitation to industrial
products and in favour of closer relations with the Six, as the
spectre of an inward-looking common agricultural policy
assumed more solid shape.

Whatever the reservations of the other Efta partners, they

were relatively insignificant compared with the diplomatic
schizophrenia of Britain's European policy, for even after throw-
ing its lot on the side of Efta Britain's attitude remained highly
ambiguous. The British government was fully justified in stressing the dangers of a trade split in Europe—but the establishment of the Seven on a basis explicitly rejected by the Common
Market countries was bound to make this danger much more
real. Britain's declared aim of convincing the Six of the baseless-
ness of their objections by demonstrating the success of Efta
must have struck them as unwarranted arrogance, for while the
EEC was a going concern with considerable attraction for some
of the Efta countries, the new organization showed few signs
of robust vitality.

The British government therefore gradually came to the un-
palatable conclusion that, for purposes of economic strategy
and commercial policy, Efta was far too slight a lever to prize
open the doors of the European citadel. This conclusion was
powerfully, and indeed brutally, reinforced by the *volte face* in
American trade policy towards European integration which
transformed Efta into an obstacle for British policy rather than
an instrument for its realization.

The consolidation of the EEC coincided with the emergence
of a dollar gap in reverse, the outflow of large funds from the
United States to Europe, and above all to Western Germany
whose combination of an export surplus, large dollar receipts
for the maintenance of American troops and a determination to
hoard rather than to invest foreign earnings proved too much
for the financial stability of the Western world. The result was
a paradoxical *de facto* alliance between France and the United
States to block Britain's attempts at using Efta for the original
purpose of the European Free Trade Area concept. France
accepted the risks of the Common Market because of its compensations for French interests, and its confidence in its ability
to defend them within the framework of the Community, but
it was adamant in opposition to Britain's demand for a Free
Trade Area between the two blocks which appealed to Benelux
and some German interests. On a different plane, the United
States was willing to accept continued discrimination against
American goods up to a point as a necessary price for the
political advantages of a united Europe as a bulwark against
the Soviet Union. However, with the American balance of pay-

ments deficit assuming dangerous proportions, the American administration turned definitely against the British plan which would have prevented discrimination against British goods by widening the trading area discriminating against American goods. The blessing given by President Eisenhower at Bermuda to Common Market and Free Trade Area alike in the name of trade liberalization turned into a veto on their amalgamation in the name of GATT.

The sorry tale of strategic misconception and practical mismanagement in Britain's approach to European integration cannot be told in detail until the archives are opened to the historian, and no good purpose would be served by retracing the time table of events. Having explained for almost five years why Britain could not join the EEC, having sponsored and sustained an alternative solution while deploring the absolute necessity of this step, the British government apparently decided in the spring of 1961 on a complete reversal of policy as the only way out of a steadily deteriorating position. On July 31, 1961, the Prime Minister informed the House of Commons of the Government's decision, in the words of the official communication, 'to open negotiations with a view to acceding to the Treaty of Rome'.

Despite this cautious approach it was clear that a far-reaching decision of principle had been taken; and despite the repeated emphasis on Britain's over-riding concern with the political dangers of a split between the two European trade blocks it was widely, and probably correctly, assumed that this action had been prompted by the chronic weakness of the economic position of the country, which had just been demonstrated by a massive run on sterling and by a sharply restrictionist emergency budget.

To appraise the causes and the effects of this momentous step it is necessary to look more closely at the economic and strategic policies responsible for Britain's plight and for the decision to stake its future on entry into the EEC.

IV

BRITAIN ON THE BRINK

(1) HANGOVER POLICIES

Historical continuity for a nation, like longevity for the individual, is a gift for which a great price is exacted. To survive many trials makes survival cherished above everything and change suspect. In such a climate vested interests flourish in every sphere, and their rule over society is matched by their sway over policies and the theories on which they are based.

During the last ten years Britain has been governed by a succession of Conservative governments, but it would be at best a half-truth to account for the relative decline in Britain's economic standing during this period in terms of party politics. Some of the most characteristic weaknesses of British post-war policy are, of course, those of the ruling party but others were inherited by the Tories from their Labour predecessors in office, including the long-term effects of the 1949 devaluation of the pound sterling, a more than half ineffective system of currency control and a military policy totally out of keeping with the capabilities of the British economy.

A detailed analysis of the British economy is neither possible nor necessary in the present context; its defects have come in for a great deal of criticism during the last few years, and the virtues of economic growth are now universally accepted. This may be due as much to its palpable connection with stock exchange values as to any other single reason: with share prices in the doldrums for more than two years, the supreme attraction of growth prospects in stocks has predisposed business in favour of growth at almost any price and it has, therefore, become correspondingly less popular to equate stagnation and stability.

In order to judge the possible consequences of Britain's entry into the European Economic Community some discussion of the basic causes of the present predicament is, however, unavoidable, because they are no less relevant for the future, whatever the outcome of the negotiations between Britain and the Six. This applies, above all, to the economic aspects of military policy, to the financial and commercial policy of the 1950s and to the economic consequences of the internal social and political balance.

Armament Economics

Britain's decline from its dominant mid-nineteenth century position, though serious, has not been catastrophic; in particular it has so far been spared the almost universal fate of once-leading powers: violent dethronement through military defeat. On the contrary, in the two world wars of the first half of the twentieth century Britain was the linch pin of the victorious coalitions, in the last war in exceptionally testing circumstances. At its end Britain was the country with, perhaps after Russia, the most complete system of war economy with a very large and comprehensive armaments industry in relation to its material resources and a correspondingly far-flung network of areas of military influence in relation to its manpower.

The hangover of these world power complexes has remained one of the most persistent factors in Britain's post-war policy and has burdened the economy with intolerable handicaps, for the official determination to maintain a position of independent military power with all the weapons in the modern arsenal continues to affect the British economy long after this policy has proved impracticable. Its consequences have been particularly serious since the Korean war and the intensification of the cold war which was accompanied by large-scale rearmament with American help and at least partly under American pressure.

Western economists have paid more attention to the economic effects of disarmament than to those of armaments, while Soviet economists have demonstrated to their own satisfaction that the economic function of armaments under capitalism is simply to counteract its trend towards chronic under-consumption. Yet the crucial economic aspect of large-scale armament may well be its inhibiting effect on economic growth.

It is arguable that even the relatively unsatisfactory performance of the American economy during the later 1950s has been mainly the result of the disproportionate claims of rearmament on such important growth industries as electronics, etc. In Britain, in any case, the attempt to maintain a full-fledged arms industry has imposed a growing strain on industrial development and the balance of payments. To spend huge sums on the maintenance of large numbers of unproductively employed able-bodied men supported by costly equipment reduces the resources available for domestic consumption. The economic damage may be relatively slight, if civilian demand is insufficient to employ those resources to the full, but the situation is very different when they are stretched to the limit. The artificial expansion of demand through large defence expenditure contributes to excessive total demand and thus helps to create the conditions for policies involving an artificial limitation of economic growth as a means of compressing demand.

Even graver consequences flow from the use of scarce engineering resources for capital goods needed by the armed forces rather than for investment goods required for further economic growth. The attempt to maintain an arms industry producing virtually the whole range of modern weapons from rockets and nuclear arms to aircraft, tanks and fighting ships must have locked up a sizeable proportion of Britain's low capital investment. Some of these projects have rendered no return at all—such as most of the rocket programme and a disturbingly large part of military aircraft development—while others are undertaken in the uncertain hope of a very remote economic return out of proportion with the priority accorded them; on the most charitable interpretation this applies to the atomic power programme which is closely linked to military nuclear engineering.

In economic terms, a modern armaments industry absorbs huge sums of capital in relation to output which is subject to unusually rapid technological obsolescence; in addition it swallows large and extremely scarce human resources in arms research and development which competes directly, and with superior powers of attraction, with economically productive uses; for a country in the position of post-war Britain to pursue the will-o-the-wisp of arms self-sufficiency is therefore, by itself an almost infallible recipe for economic decline.

The only economic justification for such a use of desperately short resources would be the export in bulk of the resulting output; however undesirable politically, such export trade in arms—particularly to Germany—is obviously very attractive, but in practice it has proved relatively insignificant because of superior American competition; as it has been used as a bait to prevent a drastic cut in Britain's military expenditure in Germany it may well have contributed even further to the drain on Britain's economic resources.

A comparison with Germany is apposite in another way as well. Germany not only illustrates the possibility of economic growth of a very high order without any assistance from a large armament industry; in fact German official policy has expressly rejected reliance on such an industry which has played a notorious part in earlier German history: 'The development of a home armaments industry raises serious doubts both in respect of savings and in respect of the enormous investments required for such production. What is invested here cannot be invested elsewhere in the national economy . . . No country should be possessed by the ambition to achieve self-sufficiency in armaments . . . Once the national armaments industry . . . demands to be heard, it will become more difficult to ban the spirit of autarky. To renounce home production, and the necessity arising from it, for heavy equipment, would also be an excellent means to reduce our trade and payments surpluses.[1] In other words, in modern conditions it pays better for an industrial country to invest heavily in productive industry, to compete successfully in world markets and to use some of the proceeds of its exports to buy arms from countries which have incurred the high costs involved in a large armament industry; to judge by Germany's experience, this policy pays dividends not only in hard cash but also in political power.

By contrast, a large armaments industry not only saps the growth of productive investment, which is the source of success in world markets, but is a burden on the balance of payments through the import component of its output. In the case of Britain, however, an even greater outflow of currency reserves is caused by political decisions out of tune with economic resources.

The string of British bases from the West Indies to Singapore is now widely regarded as a problematical strategic asset and a

---

[1] Erhard, *Prosperity through Competition*, pp. 201f.

H

very definite financial liability. But the most embarrassing item in the steady drain of military expenditure on the balance of payments is the huge foreign exchange cost of over £70m. per year caused by the British Army of the Rhine.

Under the impeccable slogan of 'no discrimination' Germany has managed to get rid of 'support costs' for the ex-occupation forces of the ex-victors and to transform its moral fervour into large dollar and sterling earnings from its new allies. An essential element in this paradoxical situation was Britain's commitment in 1954, after the *debacle* of the European Defence Community, to keep permanent forces in Germany; though in the meantime this has become almost equally embarrassing from the military and from the financial angle, all attempts to shake off this incubus have so far proved abortive. The spectacle of Britain tumbling from one exchange crisis to another while doing its bit towards increasing the swollen exchange reserves of Western Germany would be funny, if it were not so desperately serious; and the sequence of certificates of need from NATO and the half-contemptuous promise of a few more German arms orders is a grim comment on the policies which have engendered such results.

The consequences are as specific in terms of the British balance of payments as they are politically sterile. During the early 1950s the direct exchange cost of Britain's military overseas expenditure was generally balanced by 'defence aid' from the United States and the expenditure of American and Canadian forces in Britain, as well as by 'offshore sales' to the USA, but from 1958 onwards a large and still growing deficit has arisen:

Table IX

British Military Overseas Expenditure (£m)

	Total Net Payments	Defence Aid	Forces Expenditure and Offshore Sales	Net Expenditure
Av. 1951-55	144	62	72	10
1956	179	26	119	34
1957	163	21	130	12
1958	173	3	42	128
1959	159	—	29	130
1960	199	—	34	165
1961	219	—	32	187

Sources: *UK Balance of Payments 1946/57* (1959) p. 50
dtto. 1958-61 (1961) p. 15, *dtto. 1959/61* (1962) p. 15

As the 'net payments' since 1958 take account of small credits from the sterling area for which earlier details are not available, this table may somewhat understate the increase in the financial burden incurred in recent years, but even as they stand these amounts have been a serious drain on inadequate reserves. The United States may finance much larger foreign military expenditure by the credit balance of its trading account, and even so it only needed the temporary contraction of its export surplus in 1958-9 to produce a dollar crisis. Britain, on the other hand, has traditionally relied on its invisible income in order to cover its import surplus and to leave room for overseas investment; the foreign exchange loss caused by military commitments abroad thus impedes a balancing process which is literally vital for Britain's economic survival without any worthwhile political and military compensations. This permanent sapping of Britain's economic resources through a misconceived strategy can be most plausibly explained as a continuing reflex to the Great Power stimulus of the receding past.

In addition, the last decade also witnessed a number of colonial wars which wasted a large total of material resources, though luckily relatively few lives. The 'emergencies' in Malaya and Kenya, Suez and Cyprus either preceded or followed the achievement of independence from British rule. Within a cold war setting, the stamping out of Communist or merely rebellious guerillas in order to hand over power to moderate nationalists had an obvious political appeal, but the cost of this process has added sensibly to the heavy extra-economic burdens which Britain's economy had to carry since the war.

Sterling and Foreign Trade

The standing of a country's currency in the foreign exchange market is a shorthand symbol for complex economic, financial and political relationships, and may react in turn on its internal affairs. This applies particularly to sterling, even though it is no longer the leading world currency which it was until 1914. It is, therefore, inevitable that 'the strength of the pound' should play an important part in Britain's economic policy.

This problem is linked through the existence of the sterling area with the Commonwealth, although Canada is not in the sterling area and some non-Commonwealth and ex-Commonwealth countries still belong to it. Britain's continuing function

as banker for the sterling area makes the destinies of the pound
a matter of direct financial interest to its other members whose
currency reserves consist largely of their London balances, while
they are vitally interested in it from a commercial angle because
of the importance of the British market for their produce.

During the immediate post-war period, the great advantage
of the sterling area was its usefulness as a clearing device which
prevented the need for bilateral settlements and allowed room
for considerable flexibility, while functioning as a broad framework for the almost universal discrimination against dollar
goods. The large sterling balances accumulated during the war
were gradually reduced by debt repatriation and 'unrequited
exports', but strong American pressure for scaling them down
was resisted by the British Government because of the political
consequences of such a step. For the same reason, capital exports
to the sterling area remained outside the scope of exchange control, and the major part of the £250m. per year exported by
Britain during the last decade or so went in the first place to
the sterling area, though some of it may have leaked outside.

The difficulty of enforcing exchange regulations in a varied
assortment of thirty or forty countries was, indeed, formidable
and, like most difficult tasks, it was carried out only with in-
different success; in the disastrous convertibility crisis of 1947
administrative failures had their share, the 'shunting' of commodities remained for years a bane for the currency controllers
and some member countries were notorious for the existence of
'gaps' in the control arrangements. Whatever the contribution
of official incompetence to this state of affairs, it was inherently
unsatisfactory for such a complex organism and supported the
pressure for a return to a free currency system kept up from
outside by the Americans and advocated by influential quarters
in the City of London.

With the erosion of Britain's large investment income
through the war and its after-effects, with capital exports resumed on a substantial scale accompanied by meagre remittances
to the United Kingdom, because British companies preferred to
plough back their profits abroad, with the traditional pre-
eminence of British merchant shipping gone for good, the British
balance of payments was, however, not in a fit state for such a
policy. In fact, the gradual transition towards currency convertibility for current payments took place against an alarming

deterioration in the invisible transactions between the United Kingdom and foreign countries. To a probably minor extent this was the result of this policy itself, but its basic causes were to be found in the spheres of shipping, military expenditure, foreign travel and high interest and profit remittances. The following table shows the main elements of this process and incidentally reveals the extent to which Britain's creditor position in this field depends on its large surplus with the overseas sterling area, despite the heavy expenditure on bases and other military purposes.

Table X

United Kingdom Invisible Transactions (net)
(£m)

	1953	1957	1958	1959	1960	1961
Government transactions:						
£ area	—109	—155	—167	—177	—205	—235
Others	53	11	—56	—56	—79	—102
Shipping:						
£ area	104	117	100	93	98	103
Others	30	—44	—50	—90	—154	—153
Interest, Profits, "Others":						
£ area	272	341	357	358	405	394
Others	53	47	123	115	59	74
Travel, Migrants, etc:						
£ area	1	—8	1	6	22	33
Others	—6	—53	—23	—30	—43	—49
Total:						
£ area	268	295	291	280	320	295
Others	130	—39	—6	—61	—217	—230
Grand Total	*398*	*256*	*285*	*219*	*103*	*65*

Note: minus sign denotes excess of payments over receipts

Sources: 1953—*UK Balance of Payments, 1946-1957*
1957—*dtto, 1956-1959*
1958—*dtto, 1958-1961*
1959-61—*dtto, 1959-1961*

The contrast between the remarkably steady surplus earned in the overseas sterling area and the fluctuating and recently disastrously unfavourable balance of payments on invisible account with foreign countries cannot be over-emphasized.

In order to build up adequate reserves for the pound and to finance capital exports, there was only one way of keeping the British balance of payments on an even keel: a large export surplus. The official figure of £350-400m. per year as target for this purpose was, if anything, on the modest side, particularly since the growth of a large deficit on military account. In view of Britain's traditional import surplus this was, of course, a formidable task and despite a far from unimpressive export record a combination of circumstances made its attainment increasingly more difficult during the 1950s, just when the policy of currency convertibility and the emergence of a large deficit on invisible account with foreign countries made it more necessary than ever.

The reason was mainly the re-entry of the continental industrial countries and of Japan into the export race, after they had been temporarily knocked out by the war. They competed with great vigour, with modern plant and, in the case of France, on terms improved by two devaluations, while the United States continued to run a large export surplus. Although Britain participated in the general expansion of world trade, its exports of manufactured goods grew at a much slower pace than those of its rivals.

Perhaps the most frequently repeated statement about the causes of Britain's unsatisfactory export performance is the claim that it is too dependent on exports to the sterling area where imports are increasing only very slowly. Like most catch phrases this assertion contains a grain of truth which may make it more seriously misleading than a direct falsehood. As the subject is directly relevant for an answer to the question which direction British foreign trade should choose in future, it deserves a closer look.

Table XI

Rise in exports of manufactures—UK, the Six and "World"
(Percentage increase 1960 over 1954)

Exports to:				Exports by:			
	UK	Ger- many	France	Italy	Nether- lands	Bel- gium	'World'
OEEC area	39	124	134	212	117	86	109
including UK	—	175	105	224	105	83	134
EEC	58	139	173	302	148	106	131
outer EFTA	27	118	108	149	75	33	100
USA	140	231	216	283	32	93	104
Canada	71	188	173	329	100	70	49
Latin America	52	36	5	65	9	17	15
Overseas £ area	12	125	109	100	23	17	48
Others	97	179	57	220	75	43	85
Total	*38*	*129*	*87*	*185*	*86*	*70*	*75*

Source: *Board of Trade Journal*, 29 Sept. 61

The most interesting feature of Britain's export performance during this period is its success in the dollar area—the USA, Canada and Latin America—as well as in 'other' markets; although British exports expanded on average only at half the rate of those of the main industrial nations as a whole, exports to the Americas exceeded the average by a considerable margin, with a particularly steep rise for Latin America which was in some respects the most difficult market with the lowest rate of overall expansion.

These results contrast strangely with the simply disastrous record of exports to the overseas sterling area, and show up the pseudo-explanation that this was due to the slow overall growth of this market. During 1954-60, total exports of manufactures by the main exporters to the overseas sterling area rose much more than those to Latin America and at about the same rate as those to Canada, where Britain competed with considerable success. In fact, the comparison between 1954 and 1960 understates the extent of Britain's failure in the sterling area markets, for the total net rise in British exports took place at the beginning of the period, while the other exporters increased their sales in every year except 1958. Between 1957 and 1960, British manufactured exports to this region actually fell by $94m. (£34m.), while those of the other countries rose by $882m. (£315m.). Thus it was less the total behaviour of the market than that of its British component which was on trial and failed:

Table XII
Main Exporters' overseas sterling area sales of manufactures

Country	per cent increase 1960 over 1954	per cent share of market 1954	1960	change
UK	12	59	44	—15
Germany	125	7	11	4
France	109	2	3	1
Italy	100	2	3	1
Netherlands	23	2	2	—
Belgium	17	3	2	—1
Sweden	68	1	2	1
Switzerland	86	2	2	—
USA	95	12	16	4
Canada	104	2	3	1
Japan	136	8	12	4
Total	48	100	100	—

calculated from *Board of Trade Journal*

Apart from such relatively trifling suppliers as the Benelux countries, only Britain's share fell, but by no less than a quarter of its earlier total and one-seventh of the total market, or more than the whole 1954 share of the United States. The main beneficiaries of this decline were (in almost equal proportions of the total market) Germany, the USA and Japan. To play down the growth potential of markets where Japan, Germany, France and Italy at least doubled their (admittedly small) exports of manufactures in six years, while America almost doubled its quite substantial sales is obvious nonsense; to claim that British exporters were unable to maintain themselves in markets which they had made peculiarly their own for decades, while outpacing many of their competitors in the more difficult and competitive dollar markets is at least in need of more proof than it has so far received.

The truth is, as usual, more complex. An important factor has undoubtedly been the inadequacy of British capital exports for the financing of the large industrialization programmes of many of the countries concerned, though the unequal distribution of these capital exports may have been even more important: a very large share went to South Africa and Rhodesia, while little interest was shown in the capital needs of the Asian members of the sterling area. It is, therefore, not really surprising that in 1960 American exports to India and Pakistan were higher than Britain's, while the EEC countries were either not far behind or even in front of Britain.

Official policy may well bear a considerable share of responsibility for the use of British capital exports; and these normally have a direct effect on visible exports, which is particularly noticeable in the case of Germany or in America through the operations of the Export-Import Bank. Only a few months after the Rome Treaty had laid down the framework of a modest but promising Development Fund for the Associated Territories of the Six, the British White Paper on Commonwealth Development[2] rejected the proposal of a Commonwealth Bank and reaffirmed the superior virtues of private capital exports.

Another important influence was probably the abandonment of bulk purchase agreements for foodstuffs in order to buy 'in the cheapest market' and the refusal to foster bilateral, or anything less comprehensive than non-discriminatory multilateral, trading arrangements. There is, of course, a close connection between this policy and the diminishing importance of Com-

[2] Cmd. 237, July, 1957.

monwealth Preference for British exports which has often been described as a good reason for switching the emphasis of British trade to Europe. However, the contrast between the results of the dollar exports drive and the poor showing of sterling area exports may also indicate that British exporters took their apparently unassailable position in these markets too much for granted and suffered for their complacency.

Finally, the slowing down of economic expansion in Britain after 1955 affected the demand for primary commodities and thus added to the pressure on their producers to find other outlets, and other suppliers amongst the new customers for their wares.

In this catalogue no mention has been made of the continuing fall in the export prices of the overseas sterling area from their Korean peak, because this affected the size of the market as a whole rather than Britain's share in it. As a factor limiting the purchasing power of Britain's best customers it was, however, far from unimportant, though it had the pleasant side effect of reducing the cost of Britain's purchases from the sterling area.

While the British export record is, therefore, far from unimpeachable, the lower overall rate of growth of British exports in relatively unfavourable conditions need not have been a source of anything much worse than an injury to national pride and profit—except for the staggering rise in imports during this period. Considering that output rose more slowly in Britain than in most other European countries and that the terms of trade went strongly in Britain's favour, this development was more than a little paradoxical. Its main cause was a huge rise in manufactured imports:

Table XIII

UK retained imports by main categories

| | £m. | | | percentage change | | |
	1953	1957	1961	57/53	61/57	61/53
Food, Drink & Tobacco	1291	1467	1455	14	—1	13
Basic Materials	998	1107	915	11	—17	—8
Fuel	312	462	482	48	4	55
Sub-Total	2601	3036	2852	17	—6	10
Manufactures	637	902	1387	42	54	118
Total	*3238*	*3938*	*4239*	*22*	*8*	*31*

Source: *UK Trade and Navigation Returns*

Despite Britain's relative industrial stagnation, this increase in manufactured imports exceeded that of other more quickly expanding regions, not excluding the EEC. There is, of course, nothing wrong with doubling or trebling imports of consumer goods within a few years or with doubling imports of equipment, but with industrial capacity exceeding output for much of the time by a comfortable margin the priority accorded to such imports ought to depend on the balance of payments. In fact, it was the outcome of a trade liberalization policy pursued through thick and thin with almost theological fervour by the authorities with the support of most economists, though against the vocal protests of Sir Roy Harrod and others.

The forces behind this policy, as far as it is possible to guess them, may have been a mixture of rather confused motives. *Intellectually* it was perhaps the result of a hangover from the days when a free trade policy was well suited to Britain's transitory industrial supremacy; *politically* Britain was under strong American pressure to put an end to discrimination against dollar goods, while *tactically* Britain's economic general staff may have laboured under the illusion that trade liberalization was the right card to play in competition with the Common Market.

The precise effect of each measure is a matter of opinion, but the stubborn pursuit of the liberalization policy as a whole in the face of mounting balance of payments troubles may one day be regarded as one of the major paradoxes of Britain's economic history.

Monetary Policy and the Social Balance

The loss of nerve stamped on every action (or inaction) of the Labour Government following the near-stalemate of 1950 was, curiously enough, not reflected in the voting at the elections of October, 1951, which returned the Conservatives to office: the marginal shift which produced this result could not be described as a rout of the Labour Party, and the striking electoral successes of the Conservatives in 1955 and 1959 altered the internal social balance of the post-war era only marginally.

In fact, though twice confirmed in office, the more clear-headed Conservative leaders never seem to have had any illusions about the terms on which they retained their commanding position. The New Conservatism which rescued the Tories from the abyss into which they had fallen in 1945 recognized that in an advanced industrial society with an old democratic tradition the Conservatives could not hope to retain the allegiance, or at least the acquiescence, of a majority of the electorate without substantial concessions to the wage earners and low-salaried employees of which it mainly consisted.

Despite the close ties between the Tory Party and the business interests, the Government thus had to steer a course in line with the wishes of industry and finance without antagonizing the unprivileged majority to the extent of driving it back to the Labour Party. The recipe adopted for this purpose was an un-avowed maxim of the balancing of benefits. The aim of tilting the balance of social and economic advantage in favour of the business and professional classes was clear enough, but every step in this direction had to be balanced in principle, though not in amount, by some concessions to the wage and salary earners, just as on every Committee the predominant influence of the ruling 'Establishment' was formally matched by the inclusion of a suitable number of trade union nominees.

The political consequences of this policy continued to be favourable to the Government, because the absolute standard of living of the majority continued to improve. Although the catch phrase of the 'affluent society' has always been more of a propaganda slogan than an accurate description of mass living standards, as well as a convenient pretext for ignoring the plight of the submerged minority, it contains just as much truth as is good for an effective slogan. From the political angle, the vital ingredient of the 'affluent society' from the Conservative point of view has always been full employment; any serious departure from it would be the political death warrant for the Government in power, and though rising prices are unpopular, their political impact is comparatively slight.

This political dilemma of the Conservative Government lies at the root of the permanent stalemate of its economic policy. It is committed to foreign and military courses of action which impose a heavy burden on the country and, above all, on the balance of payments. It is committed to a commercial policy which prevents the use of the obvious measures for putting its international accounts in order in the emergency created to a large extent by its defence policy—and it is compelled by the needs of political self-preservation to refrain from the attempt to get out of its difficulties by an open attack on mass living standards.

The result of these powerful but divergent forces has been the use (or abuse) of monetary measures for a dog-in-the-manger policy trying to produce by indirect means an equilibrium incompatible with the policies adopted in different fields. So far from achieving the impossible, these measures have only helped to speed up the movement in a vicious circle. Perhaps the most obvious direct contribution of monetary policy to the evils which it was supposed to combat has been the additional drain of dear money on the balance of payments; the total amount may be in doubt, though it might well approach £100m. per year, and the minimum effect of an increase of one per cent in bank rate has been estimated at various amounts from £15m. upwards. Coupled with an amount of the order of £200m. per year on direct overseas military expenditure, the burden of these two factors on the balance of payments, therefore, is of a very high order of magnitude; though not all of it is avoidable and a large part of it is spent in the sterling area, the size of these figures in relation to the reserves and the import surplus is so considerable as to dominate the whole situation.

Nevertheless it could be argued that the indirect effect of this deflationary policy has been even greater, because it put a brake on the all-important expansion of output, and above all of investment, which might otherwise have solved some of the problems besetting the economy by widening its scale. Thus it came to pass that the country where wages rose less than elsewhere suffered most from the effect of rising wage costs and showed a steeper increase in consumer prices than many countries where production increased by leaps and bounds.

This permanent economic and social deadlock forms the essential background for the application to join the Common Market. The true initiative to this step did not come from the Government presided over by the man who, as Chancellor of the Exchequer, advocated the Industrial Free Trade Area as an alternative to the unthinkable policy of entering Europe at the expense of the Commonwealth: it was gradually forced on the authorities, partly by the failure of their attempts to come to an accommodation with the EEC or to create an effective alternative to it, but mainly by the growing pressure of the most influential elements of British finance and industry.

The following analysis will explore the arguments for and against this policy, examine its likely influence on the underlying problems of the British economy and consider its bearing on the future.

(2) POLITICAL ENDS AND ECONOMIC MEANS

The argument about Britain's entry into the Common Market is being conducted from different angles and at different levels. In view of the voluble partisan claims and counter-claims of all kinds, it may be advisable to distinguish between two separate, if related aspects: the effect of different courses of action on the material interests directly involved, and their effect on economic structures and social relationships.

It is only natural that each sectional interest should try to influence public opinion and the authorities in its favour. Considering the many categorical assurances given on virtually every subject under the sun before the great *volte face* of 1960-61, there will no doubt be ample grounds for claims to privileged treatment, and even better grounds for accusing the Government of breaches of faith, should the final settlement fall short of earlier promises and expectations. Such claims are best left to the advocacy of the groups concerned; in the present context they will matter to the extent that sectional interests form part of the broader picture, but attention will be focussed on the main features of that picture which emerges from the attitudes of the opponents of Britain's entry into the Common Market, of the advocates of 'joining Europe' and of the Government.

The opponents of British membership in the EEC, ranging from the political extreme Right to the far Left, have relied mainly on political arguments, such as the preservation of political sovereignty (including the right to an independent socialist policy) and the Commonwealth link, though this has frequently been combined with proposals for a closer economic union with the Commonwealth rather than with Europe.

The advocates of joining the Common Market, apart from a minority of committed 'Federalists', have generally stressed the contrast between the impressive economic growth of the Six and Britain's near-stagnation; they have buttressed this central piece of evidence by reference to the advantages of a large market and the bracing effects of competition on British industry, and decorated it by sermons on Britain's relative insignificance in isolation from the main stream of European development.

Finally the British Government, once they had decided to forget their repeated explanations of the impossibility of entering the EEC, have emphasized the political dangers to the West of a serious split between two antagonistic European trading blocks; they have stressed their willingness to accept the Rome Treaty subject to some minor changes and, above all, subject to satisfaction on three points which have been represented rather as debts of honour than as demands of material self-interest: a fair deal for the Commonwealth, justice for the British farmer and acceptable terms for Britain's Efta partners.

It will be seen that these contradictory claims contain important and irrelevant issues in almost inextricable confusion and that they omit any serious discussion of the specific economic consequences of entry into the Common Market on the British economy and on the future of British democracy.

The Politics of Integration

No discussion of the political aspects of European integration can be fruitfully undertaken outside the framework of Western European power relationships since the war.[3] The following summary review of individual issues of special importance for Britain's position within (or outside of) the EEC simply outlines the political framework for the more detailed discussion of the economic problems which form the main subject of the analysis.

Although in some respects more important than the economic questions, the political issues are relatively simple. This applies particularly to the question of sovereignty which has one obvious but relatively secondary and one much less obvious but basically more important aspect.

Despite its emotional appeal, the transfer of sovereignty from the British Parliament at Westminster to an irresponsible bureaucracy at Brussels is more of a propaganda issue than a real problem. In practice, parliamentary government in Britain has had to cede a steadily growing part of effective power to 'Whitehall' which includes not only the ministerial heads of

[3] For an attempt to do this, see E. Strauss, *Common Sense About The Common Market* (1958).

the Government but, above all, its professional servants. The share of the Council of Ministers in running the EEC has, so far, been considerably greater than that of the Cabinet in running the British government, and although this may not continue after the period of transition, the contrast between British democracy and European bureaucracy, though not entirely fictional, is less complete than the partisan claims about it.

There is rather more substance in the point that the EEC involves a larger effective transfer of national sovereignty than the other international or regional bodies which have sprung up in profusion since the last war. Compared with the political and economic bodies involved—from the United Nations and GATT to the International Monetary Fund and the OEEC or its successor, the OECD—this is undoubtedly true, though in the field of defence the effective limitations on national sovereignty are very much greater. Nevertheless, there is no reason to claim that the arrangements for joint action on Community level in the Treaty of Rome are more extensive than is absolutely necessary for the achievement of its strictly economic purposes; on the contrary, it might not unfairly be criticized for being too timid in this respect. The real issue is not one of political forms but of social purposes: once it is accepted that the economic affairs of the countries of Western Europe should be run permanently on the basis of the business and financial interests now in the saddle, though with certain safeguards for the other social classes, there are good reasons for claiming that the methods of the Rome Treaty provide more efficient operation than the near-anarchy of national arrangements largely dependent on domestic politics.

The most problematical formal rule of the Rome Treaty is the complete absence of provisions for its dissolution or for the voluntary secession of any of its members. As this was an integral part of the whole conception of an indissoluble union, its acceptance must imply subordination of all other interests to those of maintaining it intact. The impossibility of orderly withdrawal from the Community makes the maintenance of the present social system, and even of the existing balance of economic power, a matter of life and death for its present and prospective members. This may have 'dangerous consequences, if social or political changes in individual member countries threaten this balance. In the absence of any opportunity for their peaceful withdrawal, the 'maintenance of the European Community' might become in the last resort a matter of naked power, just as the 'preservation of the Union' became a cause of civil war in America a century ago.

To this extent the socialist criticism of the EEC is, of course, fully justified. Although the Rome Treaty is reconciled to the existence of State enterprises, it is deeply rooted in the system of capitalist private enterprise. This does not make it necessarily unacceptable to the socialist parties of its present member countries or to the British Labour Party, but it is undoubtedly incompatible with a planned socialist society. The weakness of this criticism as a practical political force is, of course, the weakness of the socialist Left in contemporary politics: unable to convince the majority of the electorate, or even of the labour movement, of the need for a radical change in the basis of economic and social policy, its criticism of the EEC as an effective system of international co-operation in the interests of the business classes in general, and their strongest national contingents in particular, is bound to remain a minority point of view.

Britain and European Power Politics

The effects of the new grouping in the sphere of power politics are partly speculative; they depend in the first place on the balance of power in Europe rather than on the EEC itself. In this respect the fundamental fact is, of course, the emergence of Western Germany as the strongest economic force, though the full political and military consequences of this development have so far been disguised rather than revealed by the existence of a 'Bonn-Paris axis' within the EEC and in world diplomacy: 'The fact that Germany now lies at the heart of all Western decisions illustrates the changing pattern of power . . . General de Gaulle, with his flair for the theatrical gesture, has occupied the centre of this shifting stage. The Germans—who are now the best customers of the United States for weapons—chose to act in the background, confident that a leading role will come their way in time. If no rapid progress is made with the Russians about Germany, opening up prospects of a disarmament deal, the world will have to put up with the political and military consequences of the German comeback.'[4]

[4] 'German Year for Nato,' The Economist, December 23, 1961.

In the early stages of the discussion the political realities of the situation were at least mentioned from time to time, but official British policy has increasingly guarded a discreet silence about them, while becoming more and more concerned about the political consequences of a commercial split in Europe. Cynics will point out two curious facts at variance with official protestations; one of these is the striking absence of any anxiety on this score on the part of France which is much more directly involved in the continental power pattern than Britain; the other is the leading part of the British Government in institutionalizing this split through Efta.

This split personality can be observed even in the British attitude during the very act which was intended to put an end to it. In order to obtain the acquiescence of their Efta partners in the decision to start negotiations with the EEC, the British Government had to give them apparently binding assurances about the preservation of their 'legitimate interests' in the final settlement which it may well be beyond their powers to make good in practice. The 'debt of honour' incurred in the course of this diplomatic extravaganza can only be discharged through the willing co-operation of the EEC—and recent developments in the political field have made the extent of this co-operation even more doubtful than it ought to have been from the start.

This was partly due to Britain's own decision to start negotiations with the EEC which recognized it as the effective economic power centre of Europe and thereby greatly increased its political weight. Thus it was not by accident that the Six anticipated the new situation by the Bonn Declaration of July 18, 1961, which announced their intention to set up a political union. The negotiations of the Fouchet Committee showed the difficulties of this task, but their main significance lay in the fact that they took place strictly between the Six. Although it was generally known that one of the main points at issue was the clash between the Dutch and the French on British participation in the negotiations, Britain found itself reduced to the amazing position of having to refrain from any comment on the vital subjects under discussion, except for the modest explanation that on the merits of the case it would be compelled to line up with France against Holland on the future form of the political association.

Even more important and disquieting is the growing trend amongst the Six to regard the cold-war attitudes of prospective

I

candidates for membership as a qualification or disqualification, thus completing the line-up of all European countries into opposing blocks and putting intense economic pressure on the three neutral Efta countries, Austria, Sweden and Switzerland. Apart from the awkward consequences of this attitude for Britain in view of its commitments to these countries, the dangers of this trend for the future of Europe and the world are not reduced by the fact that Western Germany is by far the strongest member of the group.

Against these facts the scholastic arguments on the likelihood of Britain's moderating influence within the Community and on the value of its support for the democratic forces in Europe, though far from uninteresting, appear too unsafe and dependent on individual political opinions to be given much weight in the decision whether Britain should join the Community or not. However, there is one small area of agreement between the quicksands of beliefs : not even the most enthusiastic supporters of Britain's political mission in a (more or less) united Europe will deny that such a mission can only be carried out by an economically strong country and that Britain's influence would be fatally impaired by failure to restore its economic health. In a very practical but nonetheless fundamental sense the political consequences of British membership in the EEC are, therefore, subject to its economic effects—not for the opponents of this step but for its advocates. If it can be shown that British membership in the Common Market would be on balance a further economic handicap for Britain rather than the condition of its economic recovery, this ought to settle the issue, at least as far as it can be affected by arguments.

(3) ECONOMIC PROPAGANDA AND REALITY

The Spaak Report not only forms the basis of the Treaty of Rome but also supplies its supporters with their most telling economic claims.

The Lure of the Big Market

Perhaps the most plausible of these is the statement that, in modern conditions, only a very large market provides both an opportunity for obtaining the full economies of scale of mass production and the competitive climate in which this opportunity will be used for the benefit of the consumer rather than in the interests of monopolists, thus creating the ideal environment for fast economic growth.

The facts of the recent good fortunes of the Six seem to fit the theory so well that detailed proof may be regarded as superfluous: did not the mere signature of the Treaty give a new, and more vigorous, lease of life to economic expansion in Europe, even when it was more a promise than a reality? Was it not obvious that the same would happen to Britain, if it accepted the 'challenge' of the Common Market in the right spirit—and did not the expansion in British exports to the Six demonstrate that this was already happening before our eyes?

However plausible at first sight, the links in this chain of assertions are much weaker than the apparent whole. Economies of scale are essentially a technical matter, and there is good reason to believe that their limits are generally much narrower than the markets of any of the larger European nations, and particularly that of Britain; beyond these limits, increased costs of transport and other services and disproportionate increases in overheads may, indeed, cause a drop in efficiency rather than its improvement.

If business units tend to grow bigger and bigger, the explanation is to be found in terms of power rather than efficiency, in bigger monopoly profits rather than lower competitive costs. For this reason the faith put in the Common Market as a competitive paradise in contrast with the drab reality of 'imperfect competition' within each of the protected systems of its (present or prospective) members is misplaced, and the arguments based on it ring very hollow after the experience of four years spent on agreeing (and emasculating) cartel regulations. A system which is claimed to require even in anticipation the absorption of £200m. concerns by £800m. combines is not going to operate in practice as a 'free enterprise market economy'—nor does the practice of the Six suggest that this is the normal behaviour of their industries.

The epidemic of mergers in Britain during the last ten years is little more than a rash compared with the 'integration' unleashed by the Common Market across the Channel. If it is regarded as vital to obtain by all means maximum economic power to face the new conditions, the aim is not a new battle of the giants for the benefit of the dwarfs, to wit the consumers, but a bigger share of a bigger market by direct or indirect pressure. It has been seen that this process of integration in Western Europe was an important ingredient in the investment boom which made the start of the EEC so successful, but it remains to be proved that it is the beginning of a new era in which big business will behave as a responsible servant of the community (or the Community).

The events of the last four or five years also ought to dispel the notion that the existence of the Common Market would even out the different rates of growth in the member countries which are a cause of awkward tension in times of prosperity and might have catastrophic results in a depression. The very first effect of the Rome Treaty was to bring French expansion to a temporary halt in order to allow the deflationary medicine of Messrs Pinay-Rueff to work; nor has the EEC at any time permitted Belgium to catch up with its partners or even to reduce the gap between its own rate of growth and the rest except at the height of the boom. There is no reason to assume that the extension of the Common Market to Britain would induce a higher rate of growth in relation to other countries; expansion or stagnation will depend, as at present, on economic policy and general business conditions. The immediate reaction might, indeed, be another 'pause', as it was in France.

One of the trump cards of economic propaganda for the Common Market has been the rise in British exports to the Six in recent years, particularly in contrast to the stationary or even declining trade with the sterling area. This was repeatedly stressed as an object lesson in favour of belonging to the 'fastest growing market in the world'. However, one only too obvious fact is invariably overlooked in this connection; it is Britain's own claim to this title before the run on sterling and the restrictions of 1961, at least as far as industrial products are concerned which are usually the centre of attraction. The development of imports is, in fact, the key to a proper understanding of the course of the trade exchanges between Britain and the Six.

The following table serves to put the rise in exports to the Six into proper perspective. In 1953 trade between the two areas was in balance; in fact, there was an export surplus for Britain, if allowance is made for the fact that exports are valued in the trade statistics on a different basis from imports.

The nine years under review fall into two distinct periods

Table XIV

Trade between Britain and the EEC Countries, 1953-61

	Imports from the Six	Exports to the Six	Import Surplus	Imports	Exports
	£m	£m	£m	1953 = 100	100
1953	347	336	11	100	100
1954	390	348	42	113	104
1955	482	376	106	139	112
1956	493	429	64	143	128
1957	491	460	31	142	137
1958	534	419	115	154	125
1959	559	466	93	161	139
1960	662	520	142	191	155
1961	678	614	64	195	183

Source: *Trade and Navigation Returns*

which happen to coincide with the years before and after the establishment of the Community. During 1953-7, imports rose at first much more quickly than exports, with a large import surplus in the boom year of 1955. This was gradually reduced by stable imports and rising exports during 1956 and 1957. The period 1958-61 started with another and even larger import surplus caused by a resumed rise in imports coupled with a sharp setback in British exports. However, this gap was much more difficult to reduce than on the previous occasion, for during 1959 and 1960 imports rose rapidly, while exports recovered in 1959 only to the 1957 level and broke fresh ground for the first time in 1960, but on a very moderate scale. Only in 1961 and 1962, at the height of the European boom, did Britain manage to catch up to a greater extent, though the performance in the German market remained unimpressive until 1962.

What happened to British exports in 1961 and 1962 is thus a belated reassertion of a pattern which is, on the whole, governed by the rise in imports rather than in exports; if earlier experience is any guide, this may well be followed in 1963 by a rebound of imports or a setback to exports or both.

For Britain, the trade balance with the Six is today hardly less important than it was in the era of bilateral arrangements, and its deterioration during the last decade is outstanding. It has been seen that in 1953 trade was in almost complete balance, but the import surplus for the five years 1953-7 averaged £51m. and rose to no less than £103m. per year for the period 1958-61, reaching almost £142m. in 1960. In principle it is, of course, desirable to have a growing volume of trade exchanges with their mutual benefits, including the wider consumer choice represented by Italian shoes, German refrigerators and Dutch tape recorders on the British market. But to herald this development as a fundamental change in basic trade patterns and to claim that the rise in British exports in a year or two of boom conditions in Europe is a sure foretaste of even better things to come in the dawning Common Market era, while ignoring the corresponding rise in imports, is little short of propaganda in the guise of economic analysis.

Competition—between Firms or Workers?

The strictly economic arguments in favour of Britain's joining the Common Market look much less convincing on closer inspection than the broad claims made for them. Why then is this step regarded with such favour by almost the whole of British business and industry? In many cases this undoubtedly reflects the belief that the industry concerned might do well in a larger European market unhampered by tariffs and quotas, but the prospect arouses greater enthusiasm than intelligent self-interest would seem to justify.

It is likely that the cause of this attitude is at the same time simpler and more fundamental; it may well be the hope or expectation that by joining up with the Six British business would escape from the somewhat precarious balance of the last few years, with rises in wages held in check by a deflationary monetary policy which at the same time hindered economic growth and acted as a brake on profits.

Beyond the hope of an immediate improvement in the competitive position of British industry vis-à-vis the industry of the Six may well lie the hope that entry into the EEC would help to change the position of British employers vis-à-vis their workmen. Within days of the announcement that the British Government had decided to open negotiations with the Six, the British Employers' Federation expressed the belief that the new dispensation would cause radical changes in the climate of collective bargaining. At present, wage increases affected all firms in an industry equally and therefore did not worsen their competitive standing, but 'direct competition with continental countries would put increases in incomes not preceded by increases in productivity out of the question. They would simply hand over markets to foreigners'.[5]

This statement may provide a clue to the rational root beneath the otherwise patently unrealistic belief in the rule of competition in an enlarged European market. As far as business is concerned, this is little more than a myth, and there is, on the contrary, a very real danger that the new Europe may be dominated by a handful of closely integrated industrial and financial giants; where more competition is ardently desired by British business men is amongst the workers. This need not take the form of physical immigration which is a fairly remote possibility in the present state of the European labour market. It would be quite sufficient if price competition from imported goods could become sufficiently real to reinforce the resistance of British employers to wage increases in times of good trade and to compel the acceptance of wage cuts by the unions in times of recession.

The record of the Common Market as a reliable disciplining force for the working population rests largely on the French experience which has been no less seriously misinterpreted than the French planning system. In fact, the economic policy which is believed to have served France so well was not the result of planning; on the contrary, it was largely responsible for the failure to achieve the aims of the Third Plan on time.

The idea of planning without tears under the aegis of the Economic and Social Council where the directorial lion lies down with the trade union lamb and both sink their sectional differences for the sake of fast economic advance is a figment of the imagination. Such a body was, in fact, already in existence during the depressed final period of the Third Republic, during the chaotic forties and the inflationary fifties without casting its magic spell over their far from attractive economic features, and even the more effective *Commissariat du Plan* did not work the miracles now attributed to it.

The results which have been so enviable to British eyes stem from a much simpler fact—the change in the balance of power after the fall of the Fourth Republic. The economic policy which embodied and ratified this change at first interrupted domestic

[5] *The Times*, August 7, 1961.

expansion quite ruthlessly in order to improve the competitive power of French industry through a cut in workers' real wages and farmers' incomes at home and through a devaluation which was externally successful, because France was comparatively unimportant as an international competitor. The approach of the Common Market was the catalyst for this policy, but the power of the new masters to act as they did was not owing to the Treaty of Rome—and still less to the rather mediocre planning mechanism which they inherited from their predecessors—but to the change in the balance of social and political power.

(4) BASIC TRADE PATTERNS: COMMONWEALTH AND AGRICULTURE

The discrepancy between public statements and underlying facts applies no less to the negotiating position adopted by the British Government, particularly in relation to the inter-connected subjects of the Commonwealth and domestic agriculture.

Commonwealth Approaches

In the official British statement at the opening of the negotiations in Brussels on October 10, 1961, the Commonwealth problem was rightly given pride of place. Britain's minimum position was expressed in the form 'that Britain could not join the EEC under conditions in which this trade connection was cut with grave loss and even ruin for some of the Commonwealth countries'.[6] The fact that different Commonwealth countries were at different stages of development and had divergent interests made it advisable to approach the aim of preventing serious damage to Commonwealth interests by a variety of steps applicable to individual countries.

Broadly speaking, the British Government proposed three main lines of action. Association for underdeveloped countries, wherever possible, low or zero tariffs on trade between the enlarged EEC and selected territories for their key export products, and an assurance of comparable outlets for trade in 'temperate' foodstuffs covered by the common agricultural policy.

Probably from a sound appreciation of the tactical situation, these claims were pitched so low that it might have been assumed that they would have been easily accepted by the Six

[6] *The United Kingdom and the EEC* (Cmnd. 1565, 1961), p. 8.

as a negotiating basis. In fact, it soon became obvious that the EEC was starting from radically different premises. The conflict took the form of the apparently scholastic question whether the problem should be tackled on a territorial basis or on a commodity basis. In practice this meant the difference between accepting the maintenance of close relationships between Britain and the Commonwealth countries as part of the basic data of the situation or subjecting them to the existing EEC pattern. By approaching the problem on a commodity basis, the common external tariff could be used as a kind of mangle in which the complex Commonwealth system could be drained of everything distinguishing it from normal trading relations between foreign countries. The procedural compromise of dividing the area of discussion into four groups according to the way in which it might be affected by different parts of the Treaty of Rome was, in essence, an adjournment of the really contentious issues.

It was tacitly accepted that no permanent safeguards could be expected for the exports of manufactured goods from fully developed Commonwealth countries such as Canada. Attempts to find a special solution on the Community level for similar exports from under-developed countries in the Commonwealth presented difficult problems of their own, but it was the trade in foodstuffs, both tropical and temperate, which raised the gravest issues of principle and practice.

A serious complication of an already difficult situation was the background influence of the United States; it has large interests as an exporter of temperate foodstuffs and is in addition the leading American power closely linked in an ambivalent relationship with the Latin American republics; in both respects it is seriously interested in the future arrangements between an enlarged Community and its overseas suppliers.

No amount of American pressure could change the common agricultural policy into anything but a highly protective and exclusive arrangement, and the American Administration accepted this state of affairs by producing the most drastic plan yet designed for the limitation of American agricultural output. However, similar pressure applied not in opposition to important interests amongst the Six but in line with them, militated from the start against a satisfactory accommodation with Commonwealth interests.

American food exports compete directly with Canadian,

Australian and New Zealand products, as do those of the Argentine which is one of the largest and most independent American semi-allies in Latin America; no less important is the competition of Latin American tropical foodstuffs with those of the African associates of the EEC and of the tropical African Commonwealth countries. The wider the area of preferential trading arrangements, the greater their discriminatory effect on outsiders; even apart from the traditional American dislike of the economic aspects of the Commonwealth, this potential threat of further restrictions on agricultural exports from the Western hemisphere was bound to arouse the opposition of the United States.

Association and Independence

Even where economic factors would make the association of certain African Commonwealth countries with an enlarged EEC in itself attractive, serious political difficulties have to be overcome in addition to American antagonism, both within the present Community and amongst the potential recruits from the Commonwealth.

There has always been a division of opinion within the Six on the merits of Overseas Association under Part IV of the Treaty of Rome. Apart from its incompatibility with GATT, which is not in itself decisive, the present system originated in French demands and was established in the first place for the benefit of France and its African colonies and burdens the Community with a large French *clientèle*. As most of these colonies became independent shortly afterwards and the association agreements have to be renegotiated in any case, the critics of the original conception preferred that the relationship between the Six and their Associates should be refashioned within the framework of art. 238 of the Treaty dealing with association in general.

At the same time the Associates themselves have been clamouring loudly, and sometimes not very tactfully, for the full benefits of their preferential position; their claims were not limited to better treatment than that meted out to third countries but also extended to privileges compared with new entrants from the ranks of the Commonwealth. The reasons for these demands were mainly two—their position as founder-associates and the fact that they are, on the whole, smaller and poorer than the more important amongst the Commonwealth countries concerned.

It would only obscure the real difficulties of the situation to ridicule such claims. It is, of course, preposterous to claim special rights by reason of priority—but this is, in fact, what the Six are claiming *vis-à-vis* Britain by insisting that the bargains struck between them as part of the original settlement should be accepted more or less *en bloc*. As for the plea of poverty, it is true that the central African Commonwealth countries have a greater volume of international trade, and their exports are much more broadly based, with Britain taking perhaps one-third, the EEC not much less and a number of other countries accounting for the balance. The ex-colonies of French Africa, on the other hand, are much more closely tied to a more heavily protected market. In 1957, the countries mainly in question were French West Africa, French Equatorial Africa, Togoland, Cameroon and Madagascar; their total exports amounted to 218,500m. French Francs of which France and the Franc area absorbed seventy-five per cent and the other EEC countries a further ten per cent. For some of these newly independent small States the proposal to widen the African membership of the Community by the addition of all or some Commonwealth countries in the area might well arouse similar fears as the original British plan for an industrial European Free Trade Area caused the French.

On the other hand, it is doubtful whether populous and (by tropical African standards) wealthy countries such as Nigeria and Ghana would accept Association with an enlarged Community, whatever the terms, but it is plain that they would refuse to consider a second-class relationship compared with that of the existing Associates. Despite the attractions of association on economic grounds, the group of powers at the core of the EEC is bound to arouse political fears regarding the possible colonialist aspects of such a scheme. To find suitable terms for the association between Europe and Africa might well be one of the great political objectives of the next generation, but there is a real possibility that Britain's entry into the EEC might impede close relations with the new independent Africa and might therefore contribute to the continued Balkanization of the dark continent rather than to its gradual unification.

In such a case, Britain's obligation to contribute towards the new European Development Fund for the purpose of creating a modern 'infrastructure' in the countries associated with the EEC could produce a dilemma of a peculiar kind. One of the arguments officially put forward in favour of joining the EEC has been the insufficiency of Britain's capital exports to the Commonwealth and the hope that the superior capital resources of the Six would become available for the purpose of developing the resources of the Commonwealth; unless the terms offered to the African Commonwealth territories are sufficiently attractive to overcome the existing difficulties the very opposite could easily happen. It would, indeed, be an ironic commentary on the hopes raised concerning the beneficial effects of the Common Market, if in practice some of Britain's inadequate funds for capital investment in the Commonwealth would have to be diverted to the no doubt laudable task of providing a modern basis for its competitors within the Community.

The Old Commonwealth and the Common Agricultural Policy

Viewed in the context of the Rome Treaty and of the practice of the EEC, the common agricultural policy is a compromise between business and agriculture, coupled with a compromise between food exporters and food importers; viewed in the context of the negotiations with Britain, it is a trial of strength of two competing trade patterns.

Historically, the common agricultural policy continues the alliance at the expense of the domestic consumer between industry and agriculture (whether Prussian landlords or French peasant-farmers) which distinguished German and French economic policy ever since the adoption of mutual protection during the last quarter of the nineteenth century. British policy, on the other hand, was based at least from 1846 until the inter-war period on the widest possible exchange of British manufactures for imported foodstuffs and raw materials, with home agriculture having to sink or swim according to its ability of competing with imports. Under the impact of protectionism abroad, this concept was narrowed down to some extent by the Empire free traders who applied German and French policy to the Empire as a whole, with Britain supplying its needs of manufactures and Empire producers feeding the population of the mother country with cheap food and its industries with cheap raw materials. Though at first unsuccessful, the programme became accepted policy since the Great Depression and was coupled with assistance to home agriculture which became an important factor during and after the last war.

This reliance on overseas sources for more than half of the basic food supply of a large industrial population, though desperately perilous in times of war, was reflected in the close and profitable trading and financial relations between Britain and many primary producers throughout the world, and particularly in the Commonwealth. The British market became the mainstay of the Danish and Argentinian farmer as well as the Australian and New Zealand livestock producer and of the Canadian, Australian and Argentinian wheat grower. In favourable conditions, this international division of labour could give the specialist overseas producer a standard of living fully comparable with that of advanced industrial nations, while supplying Britain with cheaper food than most other industrial nations, where protected domestic agriculture produced the bulk of domestic needs. With the growth of protected agricultural output in most industrial countries, the reliance of the specialized overseas producers on the British market tended, if anything, to increase, although even here the encouragement of home agriculture caused serious difficulties.

Conversely, the gradual industrialization of the countries concerned reduced their dependence on British industrial goods and their value as a market for British exports; nevertheless, following the introduction of Imperial Preference during the Depression and the dislocation of international trade through the war, about half of Britain's foreign trade was, in fact, transacted with the Commonwealth, though this proportion has since fallen to below forty per cent.

At the start of the Brussels negotiations on Britain's entry into the Common Market, the Lord Privy Seal, Mr Heath, put the case for the old Commonwealth countries with studied moderation: 'A major concern of the more fully developed members of the Commonwealth is their trade with us in *temperate* foodstuffs. Australia, New Zealand and Canada, in particular, have vital interests in this field for which special arrangements must be made.'[7] The aim should be to give the Commonwealth producers 'in the future the opportunity of

[7] *The United Kingdom and the EEC*, p. 11.

outlets for their produce comparable to those they now enjoy'.[8] This 'basic principle of comparable outlets, corresponds to the 'no injury clause' proposed by Professor Benoit and means that Commonwealth producers should gain in the markets of the Six what they are standing to lose in the United Kingdom market. Assuming that such an arrangement could be made on a permanent basis, it would thus at best freeze the present position.

As the common agricultural policy aims at stimulating trade in agricultural goods amongst the member countries and as there is a large growth potential in the agriculture of some of the Six, there is every reason to believe that the opportunities for imports of temperate foodstuffs into the EEC are going to decline. Even if the more optimistic forecasts of increases in national income and food consumption should come true, the degree of self-sufficiency of the Six is likely to increase except, perhaps, for hard wheat and for beef. The extension of the EEC to Denmark and Ireland would greatly increase the supply of livestock products produced within the group, particularly with rising producer prices for the characteristic products of these prospective members.

Far exceeding these relatively secondary factors would be the effect of British participation in this closed system. The tentative remedies put forward by Britain for the solution of this great difficulty are continued free entry of temperate commonwealth foodstuffs into the United Kingdom, quotas ('duty-free, levy-free or preferential'), market sharing agreements and long-term contracts. The first is obviously ruled out, because it would be a negation of the common agricultural policy; the others are all possible temporary expedients rather than permanent solutions: even if the Six were to accept them as such, they would inevitably clash with production and consumption trends under the common agricultural policy.

Whatever the devices chosen in order to make agreement possible, no real settlement can be reached which combines a steadily closer approach to autarky by the industrial nations (with the necessary consequence of surpluses dumped outside their magic circle) and large-scale exchanges between specialized food producers and manufacturing countries. In the long run, the adoption of the common agricultural policy by Britain would, therefore, cause a reduction in specialized food pro-

[8] ibid., p. 12.

duction for exports and a decline in trading outlets for Britain. Despite the fashionable assurance that industrial countries are each others' best customers this process can be contemplated with greater equanimity by the Six than by Britain.

It may be mentioned in passing that Britain's determination to buy in the cheapest market irrespective of other circumstances has done a great deal to undermine this system during the last few years. The fact that 'world markets' have become more and more disturbed by the dumping of unwanted surpluses of highly protected producers made the use of special measures such as bulk contracts or international commodity agreements a necessary condition for the cultivation of the old relationships in new circumstances; Britain's generally rigid and short-sighted adherence to temporarily profitable but outmoded and unfair trading methods has greatly weakened a system which was and is at least of equal benefit to the British economy as to that of its suppliers.

It is, therefore, particularly intriguing that the most interesting plan to tackle the problem of agricultural trade on an international scale has come neither from Britain nor from the United States but from France. It was outlined by the then French Minister of Finance, M. Baumgartner, at the GATT meeting of ministers in November, 1961, and represents an attempt to ensure Britain's acceptance of the common agricultural policy without any permanent exceptions in favour of the Commonwealth.

The French plan is based on the contrast between under-production of food in the underdeveloped countries and over-production in the industrially advanced nations who protect their farmers by high domestic prices: 'Policies like these, whose legitimacy is beyond dispute, have brought us to the absurd position in which we have, on the one hand, an accumulation of surplus stocks, while, on the other hand, tremendous needs go unsatisfied.'

The proposed remedy is a combination of the common agricultural policy of the Six with the American overseas food donation programme. Exports to advanced industrial countries from all sources should take place at about the 'target prices' of the Six, thus avoiding the imposition of import levies, while excess supplies should be given away to the undeveloped countries.

This ingenious scheme would have some superficial attractions for most parties concerned, with the prominent exception of the United Kingdom. It would provide definite arrangements for the orderly disposal of the expected agricultural surpluses of the Six, it would satisfy the United States by avoiding any further preferential agreements at its expense and it would appeal to the other agricultural exporters by giving them an assurance of better prices in important markets and a fair stake in the disposal of surpluses on an international basis rather than by unilateral American decisions. On the other hand, it would throw a heavy burden on the United Kingdom by adding a substantial contribution to surplus disposal costs to sharply increased buying prices for its own requirements of temperate foodstuffs.

Although the plan envisages steps to prevent the accumulation of further surpluses, its crucial weakness lies in its failure to take account of the large differences in productivity between much of specialized overseas agriculture and the mixed family farm on which the agricultural price level of the Six will be based. Given the enormous scope for increased productivity in large sections of European farming, agricultural output in the advanced countries would inevitably expand, thus restricting outlets for 'high priced' exports by the overseas producers. This would either throw a growing proportion of their output into the surplus disposal category or lead to sharp cutbacks in production which would necessarily fall mainly on the producers primarily dependent on exports who also happen to be the most efficient. The mirage of high prices plus over-production would end with higher output by high-cost producers and shrinking markets for low-cost producers.

At the same time, such a scheme would be practically incompatible with normal trading outlets outside the sphere of 'wealthy or highly-developed' countries at prices which, while well below the 'standard prices' of the Six, could be reasonably remunerative for low-cost producers. It would thus make their trading policy largely dependent on subsidies which they do not really need, a form of 'aid, not trade' incompatible with one of the basic forms of international specialization; by making the most efficient agricultural producers pensioners of the industrial nations it would create a new and highly objectionable form of economic dependence.

The same would apply to the beneficiaries of the scheme, the under-developed countries. Instead of assisting them to become self-supporting, assistance would become a means of perpetuating their dependence on the excess agricultural production of the more advanced countries, although their independent economic growth is inseparable from the successful reconstruction of their primitive agriculture.

Though the French plan has the merit of raising the cardinal issue of the international exchange of primary products, it fails to solve it, because it is based on the common agricultural policy of the Six, a basis on which no solution of the problem is possible. This fact is of prime importance for the United Kingdom, because it presents it implicitly with the choice between Europe and the Commonwealth which British policy has tried so hard to avoid.

From the point of view of the old Commonwealth, the British decision is of more than local significance, because Britain is the only open market for much of its produce. This is, of course, not a comfortable position for them, particularly as British trading policy during the 1950s has taken precious little care of their special interests, and their chances of further growth must be based on more than free access to the stationary British market. But in a negative way, this access is the sheet anchor of their trading relations in a world where protection punctuated by dumping distinguishes the agricultural policy of their other most important potential customers.

There may be opportunities for growing sales for some of the products concerned, particularly in the Far East, but it is impossible to remove the linch pin of the whole structure, the basic trade relations between Britain, Canada, Australia and New Zealand, while maintaining its external forms. The economic consequences of such a change for the Commonwealth countries concerned would probably be far-reaching; in addition it would finally undermine the shaky foundations of the present international trading system based on GATT. The dissatisfaction of the agricultural exporters with its operation has become more and more outspoken during the last few years, and particularly since the creation of the EEC, and with Britain's entry into this group its final downfall as an international system (excluding the Soviet world) would become only a matter of time.

K

British Agriculture

Despite its political importance, the problem of British farming within the framework of the EEC is much simpler and less critical than that of Commonwealth food production.

The British system of protecting agriculture by deficiency payments rather than by tariffs and quotas is in principle much more suitable for a country with a large import trade in foodstuffs than any other; most economists would, indeed, accept the view that 'a shift away from "price-support" towards "deficiency payments" methods of agricultural protectionism"[9] would be advisable in general in the interests of consumption and trade. It is only the failure of British commercial policy to recognize the effect of the distortion of the 'world market' through dumped surpluses which has made the operation of this system unduly expensive, while it has strained Britain's relations with its regular overseas suppliers. The replacement of the deficiency payment system by the common agricultural policy with its insulation of a protected internal market at a much higher price level from the rest of the world would, therefore, undoubtedly be a retrograde step; it would also be another nail in the coffin of international trade in agricultural produce.

From the farmer's point of view, this need not be a disadvantage, though the precise balance of profit and loss will depend on complex bargains involving final market prices for agricultural produce and the arrangements for the pricing of intermediate products such as feedingstuffs. As for the British economy, the consequences of the changes in protective arrangements for home agriculture form part of the bigger and more fundamental switch in trading patterns.

(5) THE REAL 'ENTRANCE FEE'

The foregoing review of the problems of the Commonwealth has done nothing to detract from the claims about the vital importance of the British market for the overseas countries concerned which were made in the course of the opening statement of October 10, 1961, in the Brussels negotiations; however, this is a rather one-sided presentation which ignores the substantial gains which Britain obtains from this relationship. As the ultimate relinquishment of some of these benefits is the real price exacted for British membership of the Common Market,

[9] *Trends in International Trade* (Geneva, 1958), p. 10.

it is essential to establish a reasonable measure of the consequence of this large-scale reorientation of the British economy.

Although an attempt will be made to assess the results quantitatively, it is at the moment impossible, even if it were desirable, to strike the balance of advantages in accounting terms or even in statistical aggregates. In the present context, the question presents itself primarily as one of economic opportunities gained or denied; more specifically, this means the effects of the switch in trading relations on the welfare of the population, on the economic relations with the outside world and, above all, on their reflection in the most formidable restraint on the use of national resources—the balance of payments.

The Rise in Food Prices

The emotional force of 'cheap food' as a political slogan is rooted in the days of British economic world supremacy, but the social and economic importance of food prices still remains larger even than the prominent part of food expenditure in the cost of living index suggests. The rise in food prices during the early and middle 1950s was, perhaps, the most powerful factor behind the pressure for higher wages, and no amount of talk about the relative insignificance of the price of the necessaries of life in the affluent society will reconcile working-class housewives to a substantial rise in food prices.

This fact makes the estimate of the probable increase in food prices a matter of great practical importance; like most such matters it is also very difficult. In principle it can be tackled from opposite ends—either through a comparison of current food prices in Britain and the Six or through calculations of the effects of the common agricultural policy on food prices in the shops.

International comparisons of food prices are never very easy, but they are particularly complex when one of the countries has a different food procurement policy and distribution system from the rest. As the United Kingdom is in a practically unique position, this *caveat* is particularly necessary. As a rule, prices of imported foods are lower than those of the corresponding home produce which frequently has a substantial price premium; this applies, e.g. to Scotch beef over Argentinian beef or to home-produced butter marketed as such. As the qualities and prices most strongly affected by the common agricultural policy would be those of imported staple products, the latter ought to be compared with current prices in the EEC; thus the principle of ignoring quality differences, which is normally adopted for such comparisons, more from desperation than from conviction, breaks down completely. As British food prices are as a rule particularly low in categories where imports play a prominent part, while prices of commodities mainly supplied from home production are sometimes as high or higher than on the Continent, the normal procedure of averaging prices in the form of an index can be seriously misleading: while there is a practical certainty of price increases for the former under the rule of the common agricultural policy, there is a strong possibility that the natural protection of high transport costs, perishability of produce, etc may cushion or prevent any fall in the latter. Finally, the method of comparing food prices on the basis of Continental consumption patterns as well as British eating and drinking habits is misleading, because the point at issue is the effect of the new policy on conditions in Britain rather than in the EEC

With all these reservations, the index figures calculated by 'PEP' from the 1959 compilations of the International Labour Office may be a reasonable starting point. They show for the United Kingdom a figure of 90 compared with 78 for the Netherlands, 107 for Germany, 109 for France and 119 for Belgium, with the average for the UK and the EEC as 100.[10] Despite the limitations of these figures, it may be assumed very roughly that food prices in Britain would have to rise by at least one-eighth, but probably more, if they were to reach the average level in the Six.

As the total value of food consumption in 1960 was £4870m. this would mean that on the basis of 1960 prices and consumption the annual cost of food would rise by £600-700m. per year.

Looked at from the opposite angle, the position is roughly similar: assuming that the 'deficiency payments' of at least £250m. per year would be added to the producers' prices (i.e. that the latter would remain on balance unchanged) and that the cost of imported food would rise by between £200 and £250m. per year, first-hand prices would increase by about £450-500m. As there is no reason whatever to believe that a

[10] P.E.P., *Food Prices and the Common Market* (1961), p. 11.

permanent (as distinct from a short-term) rise in first-hand prices would lead to a fall in distribution margins,[11] the increase in shop prices would be at least of the order of £600-£700m. per year; expressed in shillings per head per week this would be 4s 6d—5s 3d.

The estimates of rising food prices made in the past have frequently played down their effect to an astonishing degree. Perhaps the most questionable estimate was that of Mr Colin Clark who was quoted as saying that 'if Britain were to join the Common Market it is calculated that this would raise the retail price of food in this country by 3.1 per cent . . . and the rise is estimated at 1s 0½d per person per week.' The basis of this categorical statement appears to have been a comparison of the 'proposed external tariff for the Common Market, as it is expected to be about 1963, with the tariffs . . . and other charges on imports which now determine British prices'; whatever the reasoning behind these assumptions, they clearly invalidate its results.

Despite the gradual introduction of the new system, a burden of this order of magnitude is far too heavy to be balanced by concessions on indirect taxation or by increases in the social services, however badly needed these may be. As it is more than probable that part of the saving to the Exchequer would be used for a reduction of direct taxation, this would be a classical example of replacing a progressive tax by the most regressive of all taxes.

Though not, strictly speaking, part of the same problem, the question arises how far this increase in the cost of food is likely to be balanced by a fall in the cost of other consumer goods. There are, of course, certain speciality products which will dominate previously heavily protected foreign markets; photographic cameras are an obvious example. In such cases appreciable price reductions ought to be the rule. However, comparisons of consumer goods prices in general in different countries are even more unsatisfactory than in the case of food, but there is little reason to believe that prices in Britain are generally higher

[11] By making the problematical assumption that 'costs of processing, packaging, transport and distribution . . . do not necessarily rise *pari passu* with an increase in the price of food', and then assuming that they will remain completely unchanged, P.E.P. vitiate their careful study of the subject and their estimate that the rise in food prices would be limited to 1½ per cent per year over six years. (*ibid.*, p. 17.)

than in the Six—indeed the opposite is quite likely.

One of the many causes of the difficulty of comparisons is the difference in taxation systems. All the Six have various forms of turnover taxes, differing from the British purchase tax by being much more pervasive, though at every single point as a rule much lower. The use of turnover tax as an additional import levy or as a hidden export subsidy is widespread, and this may well induce the British government to apply a tax of this kind in Britain, should it enter the Common Market, even before the difficult task of 'tax harmonization' is completed by the EEC Commission. The effects of such a scheme would depend on the rates charged and other particulars, and any conclusions would, therefore, be conjectural; its adoption would completely upset any comparisons based on the present situation.

The Impact on Britain's Trade

No agreement between comparatively equal partners such as Britain and the EEC is made on the basis of a total surrender by either side. It is, therefore, reasonable to assume that any settlement which may be arrived at will protect the minimum interests of both parties. For the present and extremely difficult task of estimating the order of magnitude of the changes impending in Britain's trading system it is, however, advisable to assume that in the long term the existing system of Commonwealth preference will disappear and will be replaced, in the case of British imports from countries belonging to the Commonwealth but not associated with the Community, by import levies on foodstuffs and beverages covered by the common agricultural policy and by the external tariff for other commodities. These assumptions do not exclude the possibility of favourable bargains during a transitional period nor long-term contracts between Britain or the enlarged Community and some of the countries concerned, but for an estimate of the potential impact of the new system it is the long-term situation that matters most.

Conversely it is clear that British exports to the Commonwealth would sooner or later stand to lose their preferential terms of entry into many of these markets. This may be ultimately inevitable within a more comprehensive system, and the present arrangements are in any case far from ideal. However, the fact of their existence could constitute an important bargaining asset, and the complete failure of British policy to make use of them in proposing a viable and attractive alternative to the Common Market while this could have had a real chance of success remains one of the mysteries amongst the diplomatic failures of recent British history.[12]

The importance of the preference enjoyed by British exports in most Commonwealth markets has frequently been played down, though not by its beneficiaries. An early post-war calculation came to the conclusion that in 1948 it amounted to about fifteen per cent on half the value of British exports to the Commonwealth; since then this rate may have been reduced by the changes in preference conceded to Australia and New Zealand, but it is probably far from negligible on average and still very important in specific cases.

The lower limit of the loss of preference to Britain would be the value of the preferential margin now enjoyed by British exports. With Commonwealth imports from the United Kingdom during the last few years averaging about £1,500m., this loss would amount to £112m. per year on the basis of the 1948 situation; assuming a drop from fifteen per cent to twelve per cent in view of the decline in preference margins since then on half British exports to the Commonwealth, the loss would be of the order of £90m. This figure does not represent a loss of trade, but simply the deterioration in the terms of trade for Britain as a result of the withdrawal of Commonwealth preference from British exports on the assumption that British exporters would reduce their prices sufficiently to retain their present competitive position against other exporters.

However, there is good reason to believe that this would not be the end of the matter and that British exporters would lose some trade in the absence of preferential terms of entry: '. . . the preferences given to Britain tend to increase its share in Commonwealth markets rather more than the preferences it gives increase the Commonwealth's share in the British market . . . there is a close connection between Commonwealth preference and the British share of a given country's imports from Europe. But there are curious exceptions . . .'[13] The extent to which the

---

[12] Strauss, *Common Sense*, etc., pp. 142ff, 155.
[13] The Economist Intelligence Unit, *The Commonwealth and Europe*, pp. 18f.

loss of preference would make British exports uncompetitive and therefore cause a loss of trade is, of course, uncertain, but Britain's poor export performance in the overseas sterling area suggests that it could be considerable and the loss in overseas earnings might easily amount to a multiple of the preferential margin.

Though even an amount of £90-100m. per year would be a serious matter, the deterioration of the trading position of the United Kingdom on the export side would be at least equalled and probably greatly exceeded by the deterioration in the terms of trade on the import side as a result of the incidence of the common agricultural policy on the cost of Britain's food purchases. These (including beverages) amounted in 1961 to no less than £1,383m. If it is assumed that special arrangements can be made for tea, coffee, cocoa and that these would be reflected in the cost of imports made from some of these products, the amount left for 'temperate' foodstuffs (including fruit and vegetables and sugar, of which the EEC has an exportable surplus) would be £1,216m.; of this total £552m. came from the Commonwealth and Ireland, £135m. from the EEC and £529m. from other countries, amongst them such large suppliers as Denmark, the United States and Argentina.

As the purpose of the common agricultural policy would be the creation of a preferential position for EEC countries, some diversion from the Commonwealth and third countries to the Member States of the enlarged Community would be inevitable. It is, therefore, idle to calculate the amount of levies which the United Kingdom would have to raise for eventual transmission to the common agricultural fund or to the general resources of the Community and how much the higher cost of imports from the EEC compared to the cost of current supplies would be. In view of the price differences for the most important commodities concerned—grains, meat, dairy products and sugar—the difference could hardly be less than twenty-five per cent and might well be considerably more, in total upwards of £300m. per year; assuming the unrealistically low figure of only twenty per cent price difference, the figure would still be as much as £250m. On the basis of recent conditions, this might involve levies of £150-200m. on exports from countries outside the Six and the rest in the replacement of such imports by dearer produce from the Six, but in view of the inevitable change in supply patterns such figures are highly conjectural.

The minimum deterioration in Britain's terms of trade through loss of Commonwealth preference on the export side and through the application of the common agricultural policy to food imports would therefore be of the order of £340m. per year, but it could easily be £100m. more and might be higher still.

These calculations ignore the possible effects of other changes in Britain's trade with the Six on the trade balance; these will be discussed in the last chapter.

The Effect on the Balance of Payments

This rather dismal assessment is, however, incomplete in one important particular which affects the balance of payments no less than the trade in goods; Britain's position in respect of invisible earnings and outgoings is so lopsided that relatively small changes in strategic items may well have unforeseen repercussions.

Table X (p. 117) illustrated the fact that the steadily decreasing credit balance on Britain's invisible transactions on current account was the result of two divergent trends : a fairly stable surplus of about £300m. with the overseas sterling area and a quickly growing deficit with other countries. The changes in trade patterns following on Britain's entry into the Common Market would by themselves have little influence on the latter but might seriously interfere with the former.

The large sums spent by the Government in the sterling area are partly military expenditure on overseas bases—which ought to be reduced whether Britain joins the Common Market or not—and partly the result of economic and other grants which ought not to be affected by this step. However, this is more than can be said about the fairly regular net income of about £100m. a year from shipping, at a time when a faulty commercial policy results in mounting net payments in currencies other than sterling for the hire of oil tankers, etc. With exports liable to suffer from increased foreign competition in the sterling area following the reduction and eventual disappearance of the Commonwealth preferences, and imports certain to feel the effects of growing supplies of food and raw materials from EEC countries, earnings from shipping services to and from the sterling area countries are sure to decline.

The position of interest, profits and 'other' items is obscured
by the large transactions of the international oil companies
which may amount to anything up to £150m. per year. Other
net interest and profit income may fluctuate between £100m.
and £150m. a year, while the earnings from banks, insurances
and other services may approach £100m. Though oil transactions will probably go on irrespective of the Common Market,
profits may well suffer, particularly if they are earned in industries engaged in trade with the United Kingdom, while
financial services are subject to the same effects as shipping.

It would be idle to attempt a numerical valuation of changes
which cannot be foreseen in any detail, but the trend is unmis-
takable, and the aggregate effect of a fall in the income from
shipping, financial services and profits may well be considerable.
As it has to be added to a deterioration of at least £340m. per
year, but probably much more, on trading account, the cumulative effect of the 'entrance fee' into the Common Market would
be the emergence of a structural balance of payments deficit on
Britain's current account with the outside world.

It may be said, as in the case of the rise in food prices, that
this would not be the immediate but the eventual result of
changes which might be counter-balanced by others which
cannot now be known. If the period of transition is spread over
eight or ten years, the annual deterioration in the British
balance of payments may only be £40m. or £50m. However, this
line of argument overlooks the formidable cumulative effect of
regular and increasing burdens over a period of time. Their incidence may make it easier to coax the public into making the
original commitment, but on issues of such magnitude it is
their long-term and permanent effects rather than their immediate impact which ought to be decisive.

V

REAL PROBLEMS AND SHAM SOLUTIONS

(1) THE ISSUES FOR BRITAIN

THE foregoing chapters have attempted to analyse the development of the EEC and the special features of Britain's economic policy and position. The separate strains of this analysis meet at the same point as the real forces which they reflect: in a consideration of the true effects of Britain's entry into the Community, as far as they can be foreseen at the moment.

The economic case for or against this step will stand or fall with the answer to two separate questions: would the specific benefits outweigh the cost; and would the over-all effects help Britain to escape from the vicious circle of recent years?

Short-Term Results

The immediate consequences would be felt most strongly in the field where the Common Market has made most progress: in the reduction of trade barriers. In view of the extent of trade liberalization during the recent past, the abolition of quantitative import restrictions on non-agricultural goods would present no problems, but duties on imports from the Six would have to come down immediately by at least one-half. The effect of this reduction could be increased for important products by the incidence of British purchase tax which is much more selective than Continental sales taxes but generally much heavier where it applies; as it is charged on the value of imported goods after payment of duties, it can add substantially to the protective effect of the tariff.

It is generally accepted that the British tariff on industrial goods from foreign countries is, on the whole, higher than tariffs in Benelux and Germany, though somewhat lower than in France and Italy. By and large, concessions made to Benelux and Germany will, therefore, exceed the value of the cut in their duties for British exports, while the opposite will normally be the case in France and Italy. In 1960, the value of total manufactured imports into the Benelux countries was $4,874m. (=£1,741m.) and into Germany $4,564m. (=£1,630m.) compared with $2,424m. (=£866m.) for France and $1,887m. (=£674m.) for Italy. Although the value of current foreign trade is not an entirely satisfactory measure of trading opportunities, it is a reasonable approximation; in this case it suggests strongly that in the biggest markets Britain will have to make considerably larger concessions than it is going to obtain in exchange

Nevertheless, as Britain is selling even now more industrial goods in all EEC countries except Germany than it buys, there is good reason to expect a substantial rise in exports of manufactures to the Six, when tariffs on both sides come down by large amounts. However, not only a comparison of relative tariff reductions but also the recent history of trade relations between Britain and the Six (see Table XIV, p. 133) strongly supports the expectation that imports from the Six would rise no less and might rise more.

This probability is greatly strengthened by the position of the Six at the end of the Great Boom of 1959-61. The most striking feature of intra-Community trade in recent years has been the enormous expansion in German imports from the other EEC countries compared with German exports to them (Table V, p. 62); the basis of this disproportion was the continuous rise in German exports to third countries which has slowed down sharply in 1961-62. An investment boom in the intensity of that which made the Six the envy of the world is bound to create excess capacity in a number of key industries, and currently this seems to have happened in steel and motor cars, oil refining and chemicals, to mention only the most important instances. Germany may thus find itself poised for a new forward bound in exports at a time of slackening demand in important fields of industrial activity and plenty of new capacity coming into operation. The sharp improvement in the terms on which German exports will be allowed to compete in the British market suggests the near-certainty of a quick expansion in imports from this source which accounts for over forty per cent of all Britain's industrial imports from the Six; as the same may well apply on a smaller scale to Britain's other new partners, there is good reason to believe that imports of manufactures from these countries will rise just as quickly as exports to them.

There is, of course, no good reason why a mature industrial economy such as Britain's should be highly protected against manufactured imports, and cutting tariffs would seem to have a good deal in its favour. Given the imperfect state of competition both in this country and abroad, there is also some reason to expect that British interests would take a substantial share of the benefits in the shape of specialization agreements, marketing agreements, etc., which might make such a situation more tolerable for the producers but less profitable for the consumers. However, from the point of view of the economy as a whole the effect of this development on the balance of payments must not be overlooked; and there can be no doubt that this crucial factor is not in a fit state for such an operation, at least to some extent as a result of the large growth in manufactured imports during the last few years; in fact, so far from helping to overcome the deep-rooted causes of Britain's unsatisfactory position, a large rise in manufactured imports from the Six would add to them.

However, Britain's trade with the EEC countries is not limited to manufactures. Although exports to them consist to five-sixths of industrial goods, in 1961 food and drink imports from that area accounted for £146m., with raw materials responsible for another £52m. and fuel for £43m. out of total imports of £678m.; thus more than a third consisted of non-industrial products. It has been seen (Tables IV and VIII) that even before the full operation of the common agricultural policy the diversion of trade from third countries to the Community was most pronounced for non-industrial goods which, in total, make up more than two-thirds of Britain's imports. A diversion of trade in favour of dearer imports from the Six in these categories would not only depress Britain's terms of trade but would intensify the balance of payments problem. Taken together with the probability that industrial imports from these sources would increase faster than industrial exports to them, this would probably produce severe pressure on the pound in favour of the main continental currencies.

At this point another consequence of the Rome Treaty may well assume critical importance—the liberalization of capital transfers which has been put into partial operation well before the time table foreseen in 1957. Since the middle of 1960, direct investment, personal transfers and dealings in stock exchange securities have been unconditionally liberalized within the Community. Given the enormous growth prestige enjoyed by the Six amongst British investors, and underlined on every occasion by the advocates of British entry, it is almost inevitable that this event would lead to substantial capital transfers from Britain to the Continent, thus adding to the pressure on sterling.

How to Deal with a Sterling Crisis

The possibility of another sterling crisis as one of the probable results of British entry into the EEC has been freely discussed on the Continent, though in Britain a veil of discretion has been thrown over this subject so that its ventilation may be regarded as an act of indecent exposure. This does not make it any the less necessary to point out that the periodical weakness of the pound would sooner or later be transformed into an acute emergency by the triple effect of three additional burdens on the balance of payments. These are the expansion of industrial imports, the switch in food purchases towards the Six, almost inevitably at substantially higher prices than those of Britain's traditional suppliers, and the attraction, whether well-founded or not, of larger capital investment in Europe.

There are in practice three ways in which this immediate threat could be met without defaulting on the new obligations which Britain would have to undertake: an intensification of deflationary monetary policies; a large loan from its new partners; devaluation.

It has been for so long official doctrine that the best cure of the inflationary tendencies of the British economy is to press as hard as possible on total demand by monetary means, that this may well be the answer of the Treasury to this threat: all that was needed, it might be said, was to continue with the 'pause' on increases in incomes until the progressive rise in wages and other incomes amongst the Six had reduced, and finally eliminated, any adverse price and wage gap existing at the moment. As even at present wage costs in Britain are by no means uncompetitive compared with Germany, Belgium and

France, this would appear a plausible theory; its practical weakness is the basic fact that holding down output (not to mention growth) raises costs rather than reducing them and is, therefore, self-defeating.

The policy of output stability has been preached particularly in agriculture, where producers have been exhorted for years to cut costs rather than to raise output. Fairly consistent attempts to prevent prices from rising in line with cost increases have, indeed, been met by impressive improvements in productivity— but invariably accompanied by rising output. Conversely, official monetary policy has, indeed, succeeded in slowing down industrial output—but at the price of raising costs instead of reducing them.

As the frustration induced by this policy has been amongst the causes of the reorientation of British industry in favour of joining the Common Market, it is on the whole unlikely that it would be continued in the new circumstances. The main aim of the advocates of Britain's entry into the EEC is a better rate of economic growth than before, and this cannot be achieved by a deliberate limitation of demand. With deflation in defence of the balance of payments ruled out, the choice is narrowed down to loan or devaluation.

There is every reason to believe that the members of the EEC would do all in their power to prevent a British balance of payments crisis as an immediate consequence of entry into the Common Market. The huge amounts involved in the speculation against the pound in the first half of 1961 suggest that this would have to be a major operation. It could well absorb the bulk of the additional amounts in Continental currencies promised by the 'Club' in December, 1961, to the International Monetary Fund which are ear-marked as much as a support for the dollar as for the pound sterling.

Assuming that the scheme would be successful, its purpose would remain problematical. There would clearly be no good reason to use a loan for the purpose of disguising the deterioration in Britain's terms of trade which is a condition of joining the EEC; this would, indeed, be 'living beyond one's means' with a vengeance. Nor would it be sound policy to finance long-term capital exports to the Continent by short-term loans; this would simply indicate that the freeing of such exports was inappropriate or, at least, premature. The only sound reason for such a loan would be the need for a holding operation permitting other, more fundamental, changes to take effect. Everything would, of course, depend on the nature of these changes: if they are essential for the health of the economy, they ought to be undertaken in any case; if they are mainly the result of Britain's joining the EEC, the fact that they could not even be tackled without precipitating another sterling crisis would argue strongly against complicating the task by entering the Common Market.

The last alternative, which is advocated in Britain principally by the influential National Institute of Economic and Social Research, is the devaluation of the pound sterling in order to improve the competitive position of British exports and prevent excessive imports. The course of events in France since 1958 has made such a policy respectable and even attractive, but the consequences of devaluing the pound would be much more serious, particularly if devaluation were undertaken in the course, or as a result, of joining the EEC.

To devalue a currency in which a substantial proportion of world trade is being transacted would in any case be a major disturbance of the shaky international monetary balance, but with the dollar also in a parlous state its effects would be enormous, though not foreseeable in detail. If it were to take place at a time of prosperity in Europe, the net result might simply be a relatively small shift in the parity between pound and dollar on the one hand and the Deutsche Mark, and perhaps a few other Continental currencies, on the other, plus a rise in the dollar price of gold; should it coincide with a business recession, probably not even Germany could afford the risks of a further bonus on imports and a further handicap on exports soon after the revaluation of March, 1961, while the other Common Market countries might have to re-align their own currencies, probably rather unwillingly. The export advantages of devaluation for Britain would in any event be unlikely to be large and might well be illusory.

At the same time there might be grave consequences in other directions. Sterling is the reserve currency for a large part of the Commonwealth, and a devaluation of the pound might well be interpreted as partial default on Britain's obligations as a banker to the sterling area. Whether such an interpretation would be fair on purely economic grounds would depend on the circumstances of the case, but it is only too easy to visualize a situation in which dissatisfied Commonwealth interests could argue more or less plausibly that Britain was defaulting on its financial obligations, and making a large paper profit on the revaluation of a gold reserve 'belonging' to the sterling area as a whole, at the very moment of 'abandoning the Commonwealth'. (The possibility that South Africa might benefit from such a move, if it affected ultimately the dollar price of gold, would not necessarily make it more acceptable in many quarters.)

Even more important, however, would be the effect of devaluation on Britain's internal economy. In this respect French policy after 1958 would be the inevitable model, for in order to be effective abroad devaluation must be followed at home by deflation; otherwise the competitive advantages obtained by lowering the par value of the currency would be dissipated by rising prices. In France, which is almost self-sufficient in foodstuffs and which had a relatively small stake in foreign trade outside the Franc area, this could be done for a time as a result of a successful political change which concentrated effective power in the hands of a government relatively independent of popular approval. In Britain half the food is imported, and the effect of devaluation on import prices would multiply the impact of the common agricultural policy on food prices and wage demands.

The delayed effects of the devaluation of sterling in 1949 on Britain's economic problems were probably greater than is generally assumed, but at least after 1953 they were counteracted by the fall in the price of primary products and the improvement in Britain's terms of trade. A further devaluation in the course of joining the Six, or roughly coinciding in time with this event, would take place in conditions where the cost of Britain's food would, in any case, have to go up from year to year with the gradual adoption of the common agricultural policy. To superimpose on this process a drop in the value of the currency would transform a heavy burden into an intolerable imposition. To attempt to 'hold the line' on the wages front in order to obtain the benefits of devaluation for British exports could only create internal friction of an intensity unknown since the inter-war years and might well cause a political crisis of the first magnitude.

L

Long-Term Consequences

This speculation is a fitting starting point for answering the question how far Britain's permanent economic difficulties could be affected by entry into the Common Market. Perhaps the most succinct argument in favour of this policy was put forward in a letter by Lord Plowden and Sir Geoffrey Crowther to *The Times* and, shortly afterwards, in Lord Plowden's maiden speech in the House of Lords on August 3, 1961. 'To be able to maintain our position of leadership in the Commonwealth and in our alliances', Lord Plowden said, required a stable currency, development capital for exports and adequate military forces and therefore a large surplus on the balance of payments year in year out which 'can be achieved only by a massive increase in our exports, which, in its turn, needs access to large mass markets'.[1] The Commonwealth, both old and new, cannot provide such markets because it is intent on protecting its own industries.

This statement has the merit of stressing the link between the balance of payments and foreign and military policy, but not even if one accepts unquestioningly that such a policy ought to be pursued regardless of its economic consequences would it be true to say that a massive increase in exports is the only way to achieve this result. In view of the import component of exports it could, indeed, be argued that no practicable rate of increase in British exports could bring it about. In fact, the contraction in Britain's surplus on current payments was only partly caused by military expenditure abroad; other important contributory factors were the huge increase in manufactured imports, the decay in British shipping and the quite appreciable cost of 'dear money'. It has also been shown that it is not correct to explain Britain's relative failure in the sterling area markets by the protective policy of the countries concerned, considering that other leading exporters doubled or more than doubled their sales in these markets, while British exports marked time or declined.

Lord Plowden came much closer to the heart of the matter when he stated that 'without some radical change, such as entry into the Common Market, no amount of planning would be likely to get us out of the economic strait-jacket in which we have been labouring ever since 1945'.[2] As the present impasse

[1] House of Lords Debates, vol. 234, No. 121, col. 239.   [2] *ibid.*, col. 241.

was reached not through planning but, on the contrary, through a doctrinaire adherence to *laissez faire* and a policy of liberalization at any price, this statement by the Labour Government's first planning chief is, perhaps, somewhat unkind but it is nonetheless significant. Its implications had been spelt out a few weeks earlier with admirable clarity in Lord Plowden's and Sir Geoffrey Crowther's letter which explained that entry into the Common Market would not 'guarantee an increase in British exports. Competition in the Common Market will be served and we shall have to learn to be efficient, which may be painful. But if the EEC will impose discipline on us, it also offers the opportunity of expansion and the two together are what we so badly need'.[3]

It is permissible to be somewhat more optimistic and to believe that membership of the EEC would virtually guarantee a rise in British exports. Many industries have carefully surveyed the prospects, or had it done for them by independent experts, and there is no reason to quarrel with their conclusion that a substantial rise in exports would follow the removal of trade barriers and the operation of common policies. However, it is just as certain that there would be a large increase in imports from these countries; if past experience is any guide, it might easily be larger than the expansion of exports, with a rise in the passive balance of trade. These eminent propagandists thus chose to ignore the possibility of changes in imports in both statements: as an alternative to a massive rise in exports if Britain stayed outside the Common Market there would be the possibility—indeed, the clear necessity—of a restriction of manufactured imports until the balance of payments made this unnecessary; conversely, they ignored the certainty of a rise in imports as an offset to the salutary effects of rising exports, if Britain joined the Six.

The true purpose of this step is thus revealed, behind 'political myths and economic illusions' as discipline and the need for expansion. This salutary discipline has no truck with 'cuts and restrictions' or with any form of 'economic straitjacket': it is the discipline of severe competition. It has been shown before that in this connection the word 'competition' has a special meaning; there is little reason to believe that there would be more emphasis on competition between enterprises in

[3] *The Times*, July 18, 1961.

L*

an enlarged Community than among the Six, and the Common Market discipline so badly needed in Britain may be fairly interpreted as a shift in the balance of power between business and labour. This conclusion was, indeed, underlined by a prominent spokesman of British industry, Lord Chandos, in the same debate: 'Here we are discussing the abolition of tariffs, and the effect that will have on both employer and employed; and I must warn your Lordships that, in my opinion, it will impinge upon the workers . . . very much more than on the employers. This kind of thing will make the "wild-cat" strike, the demarcation dispute and shorter hours with less work at lower productivity an impossible luxury.'[4]

The 'radical change' which many advocates of the Common Market regard as necessary but obtainable only through entry into the EEC would have the declared purpose of making British exports more competitive; for this purpose there should be a shift in the use of the national product from consumption to investment in order to ensure quicker expansion; there would be a corresponding shift in the distribution of the national income between wages and profits, both directly (through a rise in profits without a corresponding rise in wages) and indirectly (via the budget, preferably through the adoption of a general sales tax). The compulsion to take these steps would come from outside, through the competition of EEC imports on the British market, through the conditions attached to the loan which might be needed to prevent a further sterling crisis or simply through the mechanics of devaluation.

(2) IS THERE A CHOICE?

At this stage we have grasped the reality behind the vague claims so frequently made. It has been seen that the appeal to the benefits of greater competition turns out to be, on closer inspection, a magical incantation with precious little bearing on the real situation, and that the hopes put in access to large markets are either exaggerated or ignore the complementary effects of even easier access to the British mass market on the balance of payments. The frequent revivalist references to the psychological effects of the Common Market on its actual and prospective members may be discounted even more heavily; in

[4] House of Lords Debates, l.c., col. 251.

economic discussion they are an unfailing symptom of flagging analytical powers rather than an independent factor. The one rational element behind statements of a generally emotional character is the expectation of escaping from the need for a restrictionist economic policy, such as that enforced by the authorities with short interruptions since 1955, by disciplining the British worker through the operation of outside pressures and thereby improving the profitability of British industry.

Even if this aim were desirable, the costs of achieving it through entry into the Common Market would be prohibitive. In the short term, it would put strong, and possibly disastrous, pressure on the weakest link in the complex system of the British economy, the balance of payments; in the long term it would inevitably weaken the basic trading relationships between Britain, the Commonwealth and other primary producers and would undermine some of Britain's vital invisible earnings from the sterling area. The reorientation required from Britain on joining the Six would be so much greater than for any other country, and would in some respects be such a retrograde step, as well as being costly in terms of the cost of living, the terms of trade and the balance of payments, that it ought not to be undertaken in any case. Far from being a cure for Britain's permanent economic difficulties it would in some ways seriously aggravate them.

Perhaps the most effective answer to criticism of the consequences of entering the EEC is the counter-question, what are the consequences of staying out? This question cannot be brushed aside on the legalistic ground that the burden of proof rests with the advocates of a change, for it cannot be doubted that the facts of Britain's economic position and prospects cry out loudly for a change. If the specific change proposed with so much enthusiasm and powerful backing is rejected, it can fairly be asked whether there are any workable alternatives.

Nor is it really helpful, except for the record or for purposes of political controversy, to stress the enormous share of governmental and official mismanagement in narrowing the choice over the years to the stark alternative of entering the only effective European Community on the terms of the Six or of staying out. Whatever the judgment of history on this point, its results are one of the data of the existing situation and must be treated as such in any realistic assessment of its possible development.

The management of Britain's economic affairs during the lost decade of the 1950s is vulnerable on three counts—an economically crippling military policy, an ill-considered commercial policy and a self-defeating monetary policy. Lasting economic recovery must be based on action addressed to these basic weaknesses in order to escape once and for all from the net of a stop-and-go economy punctuated by a dreary succession of predictable balance of payments crises.

To enter the EEC before tackling the basic causes of Britain's economic weakness not only condemns the British government to negotiate from a weak position (and therefore to obtain worse terms than might otherwise be got) but also imposes on this country a permanent handicap which might well discredit the idea of closer international co-operation; thus even for the advocates of European integration a change in British economic policy in advance of such a step ought to be the first task. It is only the hope of powerful interests to exploit this opportunity for the purpose of changing the internal social balance in their favour which has reversed the otherwise essential order of priority.

Exactly the opposite order of priority from that accepted in practice by the British Government should also apply to the relations between Britain and its suppliers of foodstuffs and primary commodities, above all in the Commonwealth. It has been shown that in this field, too, British policy in recent years has been distinguished by a narrow-minded subordination of basic needs to short-term gains which has seriously reduced the benefits of the system for both partners. In particular, the problematical advantages of always buying in the cheapest market have induced a fatal complacency in the British attitude towards the mounting difficulties of primary producers during the last decade. The pressure of agricultural protectionism, with its twin effects of shrinking world markets and their distortion through dumping and surplus disposal operations, on the economy of some of Britain's best trading partners is crying out loud for a reorganization of trading arrangements through long-term contracts and other means. On a more fundamental plane, Britain ought to have acted as the principal promoter of schemes for the improvement of trade exchanges between primary producers and industrial countries on a global scale, because the interests of the Commonwealth as a whole, including Britain, are proportionately far greater in this field than those of any other country.

In other words, if in the present constellation of forces truly effective world-wide commodity schemes are really possible, Britain ought to have made their conclusion the very centre of its international economic strategy, rather than to watch the growing troubles of the primary producers with a detachment intensified by their favourable effects on its own terms of trade. Thus it is a not undeserved nemesis that the only comprehensive proposal put forward in recent years should have been the Baumgartner Plan whose barely disguised purpose is the assurance of unshakable preferences for French agricultural exports to Europe, to be financed mainly at British expense.

If it is said, on the other hand, that the construction and negotiation of effective international commodity agreements in present conditions is a mere pipe dream, the conclusion becomes inevitable that it will become even less possible in future. The root cause of the trouble is the growth of agricultural protectionism in all advanced countries, and the consolidation and extension of this process throughout Western Europe through the medium of the common agricultural policy of the EEC is bound to intensify its effects on outsiders. This may well be the true position—but in this case it becomes a matter of first-rate political importance that the hope of such agreements is dangled before the eyes of Britain's Commonwealth suppliers as the only effective consideration for the termination of their preferential access to the British market.

It has been shown (p. 145) that the real importance of these preferential terms for many temperate foods (and not only for them) does not lie in the tariff preference, which is frequently very small, but in the absence of any other open market. The consequence of withdrawing these terms without putting a workable global system in their place would, therefore, be catastrophic for the countries mainly dependent on the British market. If the proposed formula for the phased winding-up of the existing Commonwealth preference system and its replacement by world-wide commodity agreements is to have any serious meaning, their conclusion must *precede* any binding commitment on Britain's part towards the Six rather than follow it in the indefinite future. This need not imply the design and execution of detailed schemes for every individual commodity, with the multifarious technical details inseparable from such a process, but a Treaty committing all participants to the acceptance and application of agreed principles for this purpose. In the absence of such a step, the primary producers are bound to regard the whole plan as little more than a form of words permitting the British Government to embark without an open breach of solemn pledges on a policy gravely injurious to the interests of Britain's traditional trading partners.

These two fundamental reasons for postponing any final arrangement with the EEC are at the present time strongly reinforced by an argument of expediency. The appeal of 'entering Europe, is based on the stark contrast between a British economy in a state of near-stagnation caused by radically faulty policies and an expanding European economy. The basis of the great European upswing of 1959-62 has been a combination of an enormous investment boom and a voracious world demand for German industrial exports—and there is a steady accumulation of signs suggesting that both forces are on the wane.

Even in the exceptionally favourable conditions of recent years, the uneven rate of development of individual countries caused quite severe tension within the Community, and there is good reason to believe that the inherent defects of the whole scheme would become patent in less prosperous times. The examination of shifting trade patterns and differential rates of economic growth in the countries of the EEC (chapter II) has provided some evidence of the early stages of a change in economic climate as early as 1961, and by the middle of 1962 this has become fairly noticeable throughout the Western world. Britain's inherent strength makes it much better capable of withstanding economic squalls than to take advantage of favourable trade winds, at least without changing the course of its economic policy; to undertake an irrevocable commitment at the present juncture might thus easily permit Britain's new partners to solve their increasingly complex problems for the time being at the expense of the newcomer.

Once Britain has put its own house in order and explored the effects of the proposed shift in its basic trade patterns on its own prosperity and that of the Commonwealth, the chances of arriving at a satisfactory settlement with the EEC, which would fall considerably short of full membership, would be very much brighter, particularly as Britain's economic interests in this respect are very similar to those of the United States.

Similarly, there is no good reason why British exports should not compete on even terms with the Six in third markets, once the impediments on Britain's efficiency have been removed.

Thus while there are no patent medicines guaranteeing success, there is a clear order of priorities which, in conjunction, constitute more than a mere alternative to membership of the EEC, which may well mean joining the wrong group at the wrong time on wrong terms.

(3) THE END OF THE POST-WAR ERA

The international significance of the Common Market does not end with the fact that its example has encouraged a number of more or less promising regional groupings in other parts of the world, nor that it confronts Britain with the most searching test of economic purpose and political will power which it has had to face in peace time for generations; transcending even this dilemma is the fact that it challenges the institutional order which embodies American post-war supremacy. This challenge is the more effective for being more than half unintentional. It has already caused a striking change in the balance of power within (and partly outside of) the International Monetary Fund, but the most important battle field of these steadily more fundamental clashes between the new world power and the old has been GATT.

Though the GATT organization is in a sense temporary, it embodies the permanent aims of American commercial policy in provisional form, because the original design of an International Trade Organization proved unacceptable to important American interests. At least in theory, GATT represents the American ideal of a multilateral trading system based on the most-favoured-nation principle. Allowances are made for existing preferential arrangements, but not for future preferences except in the comprehensive forms of customs unions and free trade areas. The Treaty of Rome claimed to establish a customs union in accordance with GATT, and the discussions in that forum during the following four years explored its international implications in searching, and sometimes explosive, terms.

On the technical level the main issue was whether the terms of the Treaty for the calculation of the common external tariff would raise average duty levels or not—and on this subject opinions proved irreconcilable. As a corollary there was the question of compensation due to countries injured by increases in duty rates which were bound to occur even if the tariff as a whole was in agreement with GATT, as the European Economic Commission stoutly contended.

Some parts of the Treaty were, however, patently incompatible with the letter and spirit of GATT, particularly the new preference area with the Overseas Associates. Of even greater practical importance was the common agricultural policy which was fairly claimed to be an obstacle to the flow of agricultural trade. The proposed system of import levies, supported by minimum prices for some products, incidentally demolished all the careful calculations about the moderate height of the common external tariff, because the rates of duty provided for some of the most important agricultural products will in practice rise with the fall in their price. In 1957, imports of food, drink, tobacco, oils and fats amounted to a quarter of total imports from third countries into the Six. Even after allowing for fruit, vegetables, tropical foods, etc., to which different rules apply, the effective import charges on one-sixth or one-seventh of all imports into the Community may be a multiple of the rates in the common tariff.

On the legal issue of the compatibility of the Treaty of Rome with GATT no agreement was reached and it was simply shelved, because the balance of power made it inadvisable to pursue it to the bitter end: 'It became clear that any effort to force matters to a vote could serve no good purpose. If the Six had to choose between renegotiating the Treaty and being formally declared in violation of the GATT, they would undoubtedly have let the GATT go. It was finally agreed not to press the legal issue.'[5]

In the hard bargaining on individual tariff positions which began in the autumn of 1960 in Geneva progress proved to be much slower than the original time table anticipated. The purpose was the preservation of the contractual rights of the outside world granted by individual Member States in earlier negotiations. At first the Commission, acting on behalf of the Six, simply offered to 'bind' certain existing rates, i.e. to promise not

[5] I. Frank, The European Common Market (1961), p. 164.

to raise them, but after three months of bargaining it became clear that no progress could be made on this basis and the Commission began to offer duty reductions which satisfied some countries but by no means all.

However, in May, 1961, the Council of the EEC decided not to make any further concessions and the Commission simply informed the Tariff Negotiations Committee 'that the Community, confident that it had scrupulously fulfilled its obligations, considered the first stage of the negotiations to be completed' and 'asked the various delegations to state by May 10th whether they were prepared to sign an agreement finally ending the renegotiations . . . on the basis of the offers made to them'.[6] Despite some protests, this ultimatum effectively settled the matter, and by the middle of 1961 agreements with fifteen GATT members had been concluded on this basis, including amongst European countries Czechoslovakia, Finland, Sweden and Switzerland.

Perhaps the most important influence of the Community on GATT is the way in which it helped to crystallize the widespread dissatisfaction of agricultural and under-developed countries with the patent unfairness of a system where repeated reductions in duties on industrial goods are accompanied by agricultural protectionism in the industrialized countries. This system found glaring expression in the 'waiver' granted the United States in 1955 in respect of a number of key commodities on which quantitative restrictions virtually amounting to import prohibitions were employed, but the potential effects of the EEC are even more serious, because Europe is the most obvious market for overseas food in exchange for manufactures.

Despite the substantial endorsement of the agricultural exporters' case by the 'Haberler Report' and the setting up of a special GATT Committee, progress in this field has been completely lacking. Though the Common Market is not responsible for the basic flaws in the conception of GATT, it has brought them out into the open and thus created a new situation in which a good many of the accumulated discontents are now concentrated on one specific event: 'The European trading partners of the EEC eye it with apprehension and see its short-term disruptive effect on intra-European trade as far outweighing the longer-run and in their eyes speculative benefits to inter-

[6] *Bulletin*, May, 1961, pp. 22f.

national trade as a whole. The newly emancipated African territories are deeply divided by a situation in which some of them
are offered a preferential access to the rich market of the Community for products which are the staple exports also of their
less-favoured neighbours. The countries of Latin America are
apprehensive of the impact of the EEC on their own important
exports of these products and on their exports of agricultural
products of the temperate zone. Similar doubts and apprehen-
sions pervade the Asian zone."

Though the professional optimism of the secretary of GATT
disagrees with the diagnosis which he so lucidly provides, it is
entirely based on the comfortable hope that accumulating tensions can be solved for ever by increasing their scale of operation. To invoke 'the necessities of an expanding economy which
can only realize its full potentialities within the framework of
an ever-expanding world economy" ignores the latent dangers
of the continuing divergence between advanced and under-developed countries and industrial and agricultural nations.

The inconclusive tussle between the EEC and the other members of GATT delayed the start of the actual negotiations for a
general reduction in tariffs, the so-called Dillon round, by almost
five months, and these negotiations proved extremely difficult.
With Britain seriously handicapped as an independent bar-
gainer because of its pending application to join the Community,
the proceedings mainly took the form of a poker game between
the Six and the United States which found its one-time protégés
extremely tough antagonists. The twenty per cent reduction in
the common external tariff which had played such a valuable
part in the compromise on the 'acceleration programme' of May,
1960, turned out to be a highly elastic concept—limited, broadly
speaking, to products where America was likely to make equivalent concessions. In the event, the 'package deal' negotiated by
Under Secretary Ball with the Six in November, 1961, was unacceptable to the American authorities which had hoped for
genuine concessions on agriculture, and final agreement was
reached only in January, 1962.

It is characteristic of the new balance of forces that the main
negotiations took place outside GATT, and that Britain remained
largely in the background. Though under GATT all member

⁷ E. W. White, *Some Structural Problems of International Trade* (1961),
pp. 18f.

countries benefit from the result, the bargains are arranged in such a way that they satisfy in the first place the main negotiators. The simultaneous request of the American administration to Congress for new legislation instead of the current Reciprocal Trade Agreements Act leaves no doubt about President Kennedy's view of the future. With Britain in the EEC, there would be 'two great Common Markets of the Atlantic'—the US and the enlarged Community—and in order to safeguard America's exports it would be necessary to reduce industrial duties and to remove them completely on products dominated by the two groups to the extent of eighty per cent of supplies. In this respect, America's much heralded trade initiative of 1962 bears a fateful resemblance to Britain's Free Trade Area concept of 1956; it is only a little less barren than the latter in respect of agriculture by calling for the mutual elimination of trade barriers against tropical products.

The Common Market thus promises (or threatens) to revolutionize the existing institutional framework of international trade in two respects. It began by igniting the smouldering discontent of the specialized agricultural exporters and of the under-developed countries with the double standards of multilateralism. It continued by destroying the formal pretences of the GATT system by forcing its leading power to reshape commercial policy on what are, in effect, bilateral lines in the hope of meeting the new challenge.

Only time can tell whether President Kennedy's concept of an Atlantic Community of industrial power blocks will be more realistic than Mr Macmillan's hope of an (industrial) Free Trade Europe with Britain as a bridge to the Commonwealth; but there can be no doubt that it marks the end of American commercial world supremacy and, therefore, the effective end of the postwar era in the field of international economic relations.

INDEX

Acceleration Programme, 19, 22ff, 52, 54f, 172

Adenauer, Dr K., 14, 33, 73

Africa, 95ff, 138ff, 172

Agriculture (and common agr. policy), 17f, 22ff, 36, 38, 43, 46ff, 61, 64, 68f, 72, 76, 82f, 91, 100 103f, 107, 126, 136, 140ff, 152, 157, 159, 161, 167ff, 173

Agricultural prices, 47ff, 55f, 69f, 143

Aircraft industry, 38, 112

Algeria, 71

Argentina, 138, 141, 147

Armaments, 110ff

Associated Overseas Territories, 8, 18, 37, 94ff, 120, 138ff, 170

Association (with EEC), 100, 102, 136, 138ff

Athens, 100

Atomic power, 112

Australia, 138, 141ff, 151

Austria, 14, 65, 85f, 106f, 130

Backward countries, 94ff, 107, 137, 171ff

Balance of payments, 7, 27, 66f, 69, 75, 80, 108f, 111ff, 122ff, 153f, 157ff, 162ff

Balkans, 99

Ball, G., 173

Bananas, 97

Baumgartner, W., 143ff, 167

Belgium, 14, 17, 21, 25, 28, 31, 49, 51, 58ff, 62ff, 73f, 76, 79ff, 91f 94, 98, 118f, 132, 148, 158

Benelux, 13f, 18f, 21, 76, 85f, 90, 97, 108, 119, 156

Benoit, E., 142

Berlin, 54, 65, 71, 89

Bermuda, 109

Beverages, 60ff, 67, 87, 97, 102, 121, 150, 152, 157, 170

Bilateral agreements, 20, 28f, 52, 116, 167, 173

Bonn Declaration, 129

Boom (of 1959-62), 10, 57ff, 132f, 156, 168

British Army of the Rhine, 114

British democracy, 126f.

Brussels, 9, 126

Business (and business classes), 16f, 24, 26, 32, 35, 45, 54, 58, 110, 123ff, 130ff, 134, 140, 164

Cameroon, 139

Canada, 64, 114f, 118f, 137, 141, 145

Capital (incl. capital exports), 16, 26ff, 41, 66, 75, 89, 91, 102, 112, 116, 120, 140, 158f

Cartels, 31ff, 91

Cereals, 48ff, 55f, 152

Chandos, Lord, 164

Chemical industry, 59, 78, 90, 156

Christian Democrats, 14, 73, 81

Citrus fruit, 100

City of London, 116

Clark, C., 149

Coal, 58, 62, 79ff

Cocoa, 97, 152

Coffee, 97, 152

Cold war, 111, 130

Colonialism, 94f, 102, 138f

Commercial policy, 18, 28f

Commissariat du Plan, 135

Committee on Economic Trends, 29

Common external tariff, 18ff, 22f, 97, 101, 137, 150, 170ff (List F) 19 (List G) 18f, 23

Commonwealth, 7, 89, 96ff, 115ff, 124ff, 136ff, 160ff

Commonwealth Bank, 120

Communists, 66, 71, 115

'Comparable outlets', 136, 142

Competition, 30ff, 39f, 88, 91, 125f, 130ff, 134ff, 157, 163f

Congo, 80, 95

Conservative Party, 110, 122ff

Consultative committees, 35, 42, 56

Consumers, 31, 34, 69, 131, 157

Copper, 80

Cotton, 97, 99

Council of Association, 96, 102

Crowther, Sir G., 162f

Currency convertibility, 27, 29, 68, 116, 118

Cyprus, 115

Czechoslovakia, 171

Dairy products, 48, 152

Deficiency payments, 146

Deflation, 28, 68f, 81, 84, 92, 124, 134, 161

Denmark, 14, 106f, 141f

Depression, 10, 16, 92, 141, 160

Deutsche Mark, 29, 65ff, 77, 82
Devaluation, 28, 68f, 74, 103, 106, 110, 158ff
Disarmament, 111
Discrimination, 23, 30, 37f, 41, 98, 102, 105, 108f, 114, 120, 122
Distribution margins, 149
Dollar, 89, 108, 114f, 119, 121f, 159ff
Dumping, 30, 143, 145, 166
Dutch Antilles, 99
Economic and Social Committee, 16, 34f, 38, 41
Economic growth, 58ff, 68, 72, 88, 110ff, 121, 124ff, 131f, 134, 159, 163, 168
Economies of scale, 130ff
Eggs, 49, 55
Eisenhower, D., 109
Electronics industry, 112
Employers, 35, 41, 164
Employment, 42, 65, 70, 78, 123
Engineering industry, 59, 73, 77, 85, 90, 112
Equal pay (for women), 44f
Equipment, 60ff, 67, 85ff, 112, 122
Erhard, Dr L., 24, 33, 65, 73, 113
Escape clauses, 55f
Establishment (right of), 26, 37f, 101
Euratom, 15, 96
European Agricultural Fund, 48, 55, 152
European budget, 44, 48
European Coal and Steel Community (ECSC), 13, 15f, 32, 34, 79
European Commission, 13, 15f, 19, 21ff, 25ff, 34ff, 73, 95, 97, 170f
European Council of Ministers, 15, 22, 24ff, 31, 33ff, 38f, 41, 45f, 96, 100, 103f, 127, 171
European Court of Justice, 15, 21
European Defence Community, 114
European (or Common) Development Fund, 85, 95ff, 120, 140
European Economic Community (EEC or 'the Six')—passim
European Free Trade Area, 7, 51, 68, 89, 100, 105ff, 124, 139, 173
European Free Trade Association (EFTA), 7, 23, 100, 102ff, 106ff, 118, 126, 129f
European integration (incl. federalism), 9, 14f, 68, 109, 125ff, 166

European Investment Bank, 47, 89
European Parliament, 10, 15f, 22, 24, 34, 38, 41, 53, 95, 100f
European Payments Union, 106
European Social Fund, 43f
Evian Agreement, 71
Exchange control, 27, 110, 116
Export subsidies (incl. drawbacks), 31, 48
Finland, 106f, 171
Fish, 99
Food industries, 36, 38, 59
Foodstuffs, 60ff, 67, 87, 97, 102, 120f, 137ff, 150, 152, 157, 161, 171
Forestry, 38
Franc (French), 68f, 106, 118f
France, 10, 13f, 17ff, 21ff, 25, 28, 30, 35, 40, 44f, 47, 49, 51, 53ff, 58ff, 62ff, 67ff, 79, 81, 84ff, 89ff, 94, 97, 99, 104f, 108, 118ff, 129, 132, 135f, 138ff, 143, 148, 156, 159ff, 167
Franco, General, 105
Franks, Lord, 9f
French Empire, 17, 94, 139
Fruit and vegetables, 49, 55f, 99, 101, 152, 170
Gas (natural), 58, 73f
Gasperi, A. de, 73
Gaulle, C. de, 14f, 54, 68, 71, 106, 128
General Agreement on Tariffs and Trade (GATT), 19, 21, 23, 109, 127, 138, 145, 169ff
Germany (Eastern) 65f, (Western), 7, 10, 13f, 17ff, 28ff, 49ff, 58ff, 62ff, 72ff, 81, 84ff, 89f, 94f, 97f, 104, 106, 108, 113f, 118ff, 128, 130, 140, 148, 156ff, 168
Ghana, 139
Gold, 160f
Great Britain (incl. UK), 7ff, 20, 22f, 33, 43, 51, 58ff, 74, 89, 97, 100f, 103ff
Greece, 65, 99ff
Guilder (Dutch), 29, 77f, 82
Haberler Report, 146, 171
Hallstein, W., 13f
Harrod, Sir R., 122
Heath, E., 141
Hitler, A., 13, 66
Imperial (or Commonwealth) Preference, 7, 89, 121, 141, 150ff, 167
Import duties, 18ff, 48ff, 68, 97, 104, 155ff, 167ff

Import levies, 31, 48ff, 150, 152, 170
'Indexation', 70
India, 120
Indonesia, 76
Industry, 16f, 24, 36, 43, 55, 58ff, 68f, 72, 78, 134
Infrastructure, 40, 47
Insurance, 38
International Labour Office, 148
International Monetary Fund (IMF), 30, 127, 159, 169
Ireland, Republic of, 103ff, 142
Israel, 103
Italian Somaliland, 94f
Italy, 13f, 17ff, 21ff, 25, 28, 31, 35, 40, 47, 49, 51, 56, 58ff, 62ff, 68, 72ff, 79, 84ff, 89f, 94, 99ff, 104, 118ff, 156
Investment, 59, 64f, 72, 74, 77, 80, 88ff, 102, 112, 124, 164, 168
Invisible transactions, 66, 75, 115ff, 153f, 165
Japan, 118ff
Kennedy, J. F., 173
Kenya, 115
Korean war, 58, 111, 121
Labour, 16ff, 41ff, 164 (mobility), 26, 28, 41ff, 101 (shortage), 42, 78
Labour Government (British), 122, 163
Labour parties, 14, 53, (British) 110, 122f, 128
Latin America, 95, 97, 118f, 137f, 172
Leather industry, 74
Lemass, S., 104
Long-term contracts, 46, 48, 120, 142ff, 150, 166
Luxembourg, 21, 28, 49, 58ff, 73, 76, 83f, 94
Macmillan, H., 104, 109, 124, 173
Madagascar, 95, 139
Malaya, 115
Manufactures, 23, 28, 52, 61, 67, 86ff, 121f, 137, 157
Mass markets, 130ff, 162, 164, 173
Meat, 48f, 55, 152
Mergers, 36f, 88f, 91, 131
Migrant labour, 42f, 75, 135
Military expenditure, 110ff, 117, 123, 153, 162
Milk, 49, 53, 55
Mining, 58, 73, 79
Mollet, G., 67

Monetary Committee, 26
Monetary policy, 26ff, 122ff, 158ff, 166
Monnet, J., 34, 36
Monopolies, 32ff, 72, 91, 131f
Motor cars, 156
National Institute of Economic and Social Research, 160
Nazis, 13f
Netherlands (incl. Holland), 14, 17, 23, 25, 28ff, 40, 49, 51ff, 58ff, 62ff, 68, 74, 76ff, 81, 84ff, 98f, 104, 118f, 129, 148
Newsprint, 19
New Zealand, 138, 141ff, 151
Nigeria, 139
North Atlantic Treaty Organization (NATO), 104, 114
Norway, 14, 106f
Oil, 62, 73, 99, 153f, 156 (products), 19, 99
Oils and fats, 47, 61, 170
Olive oil, 100
Organization for European Economic Co-operation (OEEC, incl. OECD), 10, 19, 105f, 118, 127
Overseas bases, 111, 113ff, 117, 153
Overseas sterling area, 115ff, 124, 152ff, 161f, 165
Pakistan, 120
Parliament (British), 104, 109, 126, 162ff
Peasant-farmers, 17, 71, 75, 102
Photographic cameras, 149
Pinay, E., 68ff, 81, 132
Planning, 135f, 162f
Plowden, Lord, 162ff
Portugal, 100, 106
Pound sterling, 109f, 115ff, 157ff
Preferences (see also Imperial Preference), 19f, 42f, 86, 94, 96ff, 138f, 152, 167ff
Prices (see also agricultural prices), 65, 69ff, 75, 77, 105, 123f, 143ff, 147ff, 161 (stabilization) 98
Primary commodities, 28, 52, 61, 86, 121, 166
Profits, 65, 70f, 75, 117, 131, 153f, 164f
Protectionism, 51, 97, 100, 140f, 145f, 157, 166ff
Quantitative restrictions (incl. quotas), 20f, 48, 50, 52f, 97, 155
Railways, 38f
Raisins, 101

Raw materials, 60ff, 67, 87, 102, 121, 157
Regional development, 47
Research, 112
Restrictive practices (see also cartels, mergers and monopolies), 31ff
Retail trade, 38
Rhine, 76
Rhodesia, 120
Rice, 47, 55
Roman Catholic Church, 14
Rome, 96
Rome Treaty, 8, 15ff, 37ff, 57f, 64, 67f, 81, 83, 90f, 100ff, 106, 109, 120, 126ff, 136ff, 140, 158, 169ff
Rueff, J., 68f, 72, 132
Ruhr, 32, 64, 76
Saar, 84
Sahara, 99
Sandri, L., 45
Sardinia, 72
Secession, 127f
Services, 26, 28, 37f
Share prices, 10, 65, 70f, 75, 110
Shipbuilding, 31, 38
Shipping, 73, 116f, 153ff
Sicily, 72
Singapore, 113
Socialists, 71, 81, 101, 128
Social market economy, 32, 34, 90f, 105
Social policy, 25, 43ff
South Africa, 120, 161
Sovereignty, 126ff
Soviet Union (incl. Russia), 64, 107f, 111
Spaak Report, 130
Spain, 65, 105
Specialization agreements, 36, 88
State aids, 30f, 53
State enterprises, 72f, 128
Steel, 32, 59, 73, 80f, 83, 156
Stockholm Agreement, 107
Strasbourg, 96
Suez, 62, 115
Sugar, 48, 55, 152
Surinam, 99

Sweden, 106f, 119, 130, 171
Switzerland, 73, 106f, 119, 130, 171
Synthetic rubber, 31
Taxation, 31, 80, 95, 97, 150, 155, 164
Tea, 152
Terms of trade, 121, 151ff, 159
Textile industries, 59, 74, 80
The Times, 162f
Tobacco, 19, 60ff, 67, 87, 99, 101ff, 121, 170
Togoland, 139
Trade, (foreign) 59ff, 69, 74ff, 85ff, 102, 113, 117ff, 140ff, 150ff, 156, 162, 166ff (intra-Community) 16, 22ff, 60ff, 87, 156
Trade associations, 36, 88
Trade barriers (incl. liberalization), 16ff, 20ff, 50, 103, 122, 155, 163
Trade distortions, 18, 22, 39, 43, 53
Trade unions, 41, 65, 71, 101, 123
Transition period, 18, 20, 44f, 48f, 54f
Transport (incl. common transport policy), 18, 25, 38ff, 64, 82f, 85
Tropical products, 97, 137ff, 173
Tunisia, 103
Turkey, 65, 100, 103
Turnover (and sales), taxes, 31, 150, 155
Unemployment, 42, 73, 82
United Nations, 127
United States of America (USA), 7ff, 23, 64, 89f, 97, 101, 108f, 111ff, 116, 118ff, 128, 137f, 143f, 169ff
Uranium, 80
Wage pause, 70f, 92, 158
Wages, 65f, 70ff, 73ff, 76, 91f, 124, 134ff, 158f, 161, 164
War economy, 111
Welfare State, 17, 44, 123
West Indies, 113
White, E. W., 172
Wigny, M., 22
Wine, 45, 55, 99ff
World market, 48, 143ff, 166
Workers, 17, 35f, 66, 71, 75, 123, 134ff, 164f

GEORGE ALLEN & UNWIN LTD

London: 40 Museum Street, W.C.1

Auckland: 24 Wyndham Street
Bombay: 15 Graham Road, Ballard Estate, Bombay 1
Buenos Aires: Escritorio 454-459, Florida 165
Calcutta: 17 Chittaranjan Avenue, Calcutta 13
Cape Town: 109 Long Street
Hong Kong: F1/12 Mirador Mansions, Kowloon
Ibadan: P.O. Box 62
Karachi: Karachi Chambers, McLeod Road
Madras: Mohan Mansion, 38c Mount Road, Madras 6
Mexico: Villalongin 32-10, Piso, Mexico 5, D.F.
Nairobi: P.O. Box 12446
New Delhi: 13-14 Ajmeri Gate Extension, New Delhi
Sao Paulo: Avenida 9 De Julho 1138-Ap. 51
Singapore: 36c Prinsep Street, Singapore 7
Sydney, N.S.W.: Bradbury House, 55 York Street
Toronto: 91 Wellington Street West

MONEY TRADE AND ECONOMIC GROWTH

SURVEY LECTURES IN ECONOMIC GROWTH

HARRY G. JOHNSON

This book surveys a broad range of subjects in a brief space, but it has all Professor Johnson's originality and incisiveness. The first part deals with international trade and economic growth: Professor Johnson discusses the Balance of Payments, seen nowadays as a policy problem, the modern theories of comparative costs and commercial policy and the new development in the theory of customs unions or preferential groups—a highly topical subject.

The second part is concerned with modern monetary theory and a re-examination of Keynes after twenty-five years. In the third part Professor Johnson discusses the roles of planning and the market in economic development, and makes some original contributions to the economic theory of the 'affluent society' and the theory of its social policy—a field which he is convinced will yield interesting and fruitful applications of economic analysis.

Demy 8vo. 25s. net

A NEO-CLASSICAL THEORY OF ECONOMIC GROWTH

J. E. MEADE

Much attention is now paid to problems of economic growth. What is it that makes real income grow rapidly in some economics and only slowly in others? Political and social factors play a major role in the answer to this question, but purely economic considerations remain of great importance. Many economic theorists have used entirely new methods of economic analysis to deal with this question. But in this short book Professor Meade has outlined the way in which classical economic analysis may be developed for application to the problem of economic growth. This is a book for the student of economic theory; but the basic theory is expounded in the main text of this book in a way which does not demand any extensive familiarity with mathematical techniques.

Demy 8vo. 28s. net

BUYING BY VOLUNTARY CHAINS

AND OTHER ASSOCIATIONS OF RETAILERS
AND WHOLESALERS

CHRISTINA FULOP

This is the first book to be published in this country on Voluntary Chains. This important marketing innovation rests on the co-operation of wholesalers and retailers in buying and other retail activities and it will largely determine the future both of the independent wholesaler and of the small retailer in food distribution. The author discusses the development, present position, and future prospects of the Voluntary Chain; in particular she analyses how far it is able to secure the same economies of operation, and to make its members as well-informed as the multiple concern.

This book will be of value not only to every retailer, wholesaler and manufacturer, but equally to the student of distribution, and the investor. It comes at a most opportune moment when the whole field of retailing is receiving more attention than it has had for many years past. *Demy 8vo.* 21s. *net*

THE THEORY OF ECONOMIC
INTEGRATION

BELA A. BALASSA

This is an excellent exposition of a complex and far-reaching topic. It will interest economists in Europe by reason of its subject and treatment, but it is also a valuable and reliable textbook for students tackling integration as part of a course on International Economics and for those studying Public Finance.

In offering this theoretical study, the author builds on the conclusions of other writers, but goes beyond this in providing a unifying framework for previous contributions and in exploring questions that in the past received little attention—in particular, the relationship between economic integration and growth (especially the inter-relationship between market size and growth, and the implications of various factors for economic growth in an integrated area). Among these are: economies of large-scale production, competition, technological change, uncertainty and the allocation of investment funds. The last four chapters cover the problems of economic policy in an integrated area.

Medium 8vo. 28s. *net*

GEORGE ALLEN & UNWIN LTD